TEACHING AIDS IN MATHEMATICS

A Handbook for Elementary Teachers

TEACHING AIDS IN MATHEMATICS

A Handbook for Elementary Teachers

DR. ROOHI FATIMA

KANISHKA PUBLISHERS, DISTRIBUTORS
NEW DELHI-110 002

KANISHKA PUBLISHERS, DISTRIBUTORS
4697/5-21A, Ansari Road, Daryaganj
New Delhi -110 002
Phones : 2327 0497, 2328 8285
Fax : 011-2328 8285
E-mail : kanishka_publishing@yahoo.co.in

Teaching Aids in Mathematics
Edition: 2016

PRINTED IN INDIA

Published by Madan Sachdeva for Kanishka Publishers, Distributors, 4697/5-21A, Ansari Road, Daryaganj, New Delhi-110 002, Typeset by Sunshine Graphics, Delhi, and Printed at Rajdhani Printers, Delhi.

Dedicated
To
My Abbu

Late Syed Iqbal Mehdi Zaidi who taught me counting
and
installed in me the love for Mathematics

Foreword

Dr. Roohi Fatima is a versatile teacher, who has a long experience of teaching Mathematics in school and also in the teacher training institute. She is the right person to take up writing of this handbook for teachers of mathematics. I am quite sure that it would be equally useful for teacher educators. Teaching aid plays a very significant role in developing conceptual understanding. It is more so at the early stages of Education. The book deals with the importance of mathematics in every body's life and also for the sake of teachers to understand the areas of studies in mathematics, the author clearly spelt out the term 'mathematics'. It is strange that there is growing feelings that passing in Mathematics need not be made compulsory as it is thought that mathematics develops fear complex in students. Instead, if mathematics is taught in a natural way i.e. keeping the maxims of teaching in view—from concrete to abstract; from known to unknown and from simple to complex, it would not make a difficult subject for students to learn. And, therefore, it is more important for teachers to be properly equipped. Knowledge of various types of teaching aids and their appropriate use will make learning of mathematics a great fun. The NCFSE-2005 also emphasizes these aspects of students learning by focusing on child centred learning.

The Handbook deals with almost all aspects of teaching and learning of mathematics with pictorial illustrations. The author is convinced and so am I, that the level of achievement could be substantially enhanced if the abstractions in mathematics are approached through concrete materials.

After reading the book, I am of the opinion that the handbook will prove to be of immense help to mathematics teachers as well as teacher educators.

Prof. Mohammad Miyan
Hony. Director, Arjun Singh Centre for Distance and Open Learning Jamia Millia Islamia New Delhi-110025

Preface

Mathematics plays a predominant role in our everyday life and has become an indispensable factor for the progress of our present day world. Counting starts from day one of the birth of a person. On the other hand, the "National Commission for Minority Education Institutions" has suggested that passing English and Mathematics should not be compulsory for promotion in secondary schools. The argument is that most of the students find mathematics difficult and thus do not show good results in mathematics. According to the "Learning Ability Survey" made by NCERT, the overall achievement in mathematics for class VII is 29.78% and for class VIII is 38.47%. These figures show that even though mathematics is very important to learn there are still some problems in learning this subject. It is a fact that there are many abstractions in mathematics, which cannot be easily followed by the students.

As teacher of mathematics it is our responsibility to make such abstract and complex ideas, easily comprehendible and concrete to make the learning of mathematics easy. This book is an effort in this direction. My experience of teaching mathematics shows that students take part in the learning process; they investigate and explore, and thereby can actually 'find' mathematics themselves. For this they need some concrete teaching aids in their hands, which will give a better picture.

This book contains 10 chapters with 179 illustrations.

Chapter 1: *Mathematics for life—An Introduction.* Deals with the importance of mathematics in daily life, different definitions and interpretation of the term mathematics.

Chapter 2: *Importance of teaching mathematics in school:* In this chapter, the author discusses objectives of teaching mathematics at different levels *i.e.*, primary and secondary levels.

Chapter 3: Ways *of teaching of mathematics:* This chapter deals with the main aim of teaching of mathematics and how can we achieve this aim?

Chapter 4: *Teaching Aids in Mathematics:* This chapter refers to the concept of teaching aids; their need and different principles for using them.

Chapter 5: Types *of teaching aids:* This chapter deals with different types of teaching aids.

Chapter 6: *Real object:* This chapter provides the use of real objects as a teaching aid with examples.

Chapter 7: *Models:* In this chapter, the author discusses 39 models, which can be used in teaching different concepts of mathematics.

Chapter 8: *Charts:* This chapter deals with the importance of using charts in teaching of mathematics by giving examples.

Chapter 9: *Use of paper.* This chapter deals with the use of paper as an important teaching aid in mathematics teaching with examples.

One of the highlights of the book is that operational rules for each teaching aid, along with a description of its usage etc has been incorporated.

Chapter 10: *Other types of teaching of mathematics:* Beside the teaching aids, discussed in earlier chapters, there are some other types also, which are discussed briefly in this chapter, computer, which is one of them, has been discussed in detail by giving examples of lessons which can be taught with the help of computers.

This book is an effort to give a concrete shape to the abstract concepts of mathematics and it will be helpful for pre as well as in service school teachers for teaching mathematics in an easy and interesting way.

Dr. Roohi Fatima
IASE, Faculty of Education Jamia Millia Islamia
New Delhi 25.

Acknowledgment

I take this opportunity to acknowledge with thanks the contribution of those who made this work possible.

First and foremost I want to put on record the contribution of my students who provided me with ideas and inspired me for writing a book dealing with the use of teaching aid in teaching of mathematics. Presentation of abstract ideas through concrete aid not only helped the students to learn mathematics but also developed interest in the subject.

I would like to express my sincere gratitude to Prof. Talat Aziz, IASE, Faculty of Education, Jamia Millia Islamia. Her encouragement and moral support became the source of inspiration for me to carry out my work.

I am also grateful to Dr. Ikram Ahmad, Faculty of Education, for his valuable guidance and suggestions he provided during the finalization of the book.

My sincere thanks are due to Prof. Sharfuddin Ahmad, Department of Mathematics, Jamia Millia Islamia for his constant support during my work. Inspiration for hard work came from my supervisor for Ph.D. Dr. Shoib Abdullah, IASE, Jamia Millia Islamia. I want to thank him also.

I am also thankful to Jamia Premchand Achieves, Jamia Millia Islamia, for providing me a relevant and beautiful photograph of a mathematics classroom of Madarsai-Ibtadai, for the title cover of this book.

I would like to extent my gratitude for my family members especially my husband Mr. Azam Shibli, my daughter Natalia Shibli and son Tabish Shibli for bearing with me, sacrificing their engagements and programmes and constantly providing me not only moral support for enabling me to keep up my sprit but also helping me to develop and draw designs of various teaching aids through computer.

I am grateful to Mr. Madan Sachdeva, Kanishka Publishers & Distributors, Delhi, for publishing my book.

Contents

1

Mathematics for Life: An Introduction

1.1 Introduction

Is there any place where mathematics is not used? Think about it and make a list of those places. How many places have you found? One, two, three, many or none. What do you conclude from this?

Mathematics is helpful in almost every kind of human endeavour from laying bricks to prescribing medicine or drawing a picture. In particular, mathematics has contributed to progress in science and technology for thousands of years and still continues to do so. It finds useful applications in business, industry, music, psychology, history, politics, sports, medicine, agriculture, engineering, and the social and natural sciences.

It helps man to give an exact interpretation to his ideas and conclusions. It deals with problems involving space and form. It enables the man to study various phenomena in space and establish various relationships between them. Mathematics is the numerical and calculation part of a man's life and knowledge. It plays a predominant role in our everyday life and has become an indispensable factor for the progress of our present day world. Let us see how?

1.2 Importance of Mathematics in Daily Life

What is the first thing you do when you get up in the morning? See the time and make yourself a nice cup of tea or coffee? If so, then do you use mathematics? Try to make a list of your daily routine from getting up in the morning till sleeping in the night. Can you observe how many times you used mathematics in a whole day?

Consider a carpenter making a chair, a table, or a bed. Does he use mathematics in any way? Look at a shopkeeper, a potter, a tailor, a shoemaker, a cowherd, a vegetable seller or a mason. Do they use mathematics in any way? When we drive a car or a scooter or use public transport, we are using mathematics. When we go for shopping or pay the electric bill or telephone bill or pay our child's school fees, we are using mathematics. Sending a satellite up into the orbit, building roads and bridges—can any of these activities be done without using mathematics? We do a lot of mathematics even while working in the kitchen *e.g.*, the skills of ratio and proportion, estimation, counting, etc. are used in the kitchen. Even in making a *chapatti* we use mathematics.

Each individual is required to compute his or her income and balance his/her family budget irrespective of having any formal education of mathematics. While calculating the rates, taxes, insurance premium, savings and interests, rents etc. we use mathematics and we can be reasonably sure that we are getting our dues only if we have good mathematical background.

Even social sciences like economics, psychology, geography etc., make abundant use of mathematics. The gigantic work of construction of dams, bridges, building of ships, airplanes, bombs etc. are possible only because of the quantitative science. Even in medical services mathematics is used to measure the doses, the blood pressure, the rate of the pulse, the body temperature etc. Most of the natural sciences and philosophy are to be studied on mathematical lines and without the study of mathematics there would be no improvement in them.

And what about the various sports activities? In hockey, cricket, kho-kho, kabaddi, football, basketball etc., mathematics is used. A cricket captain once said that if he got his field placement right, half the job of getting the other team out would be done. And what does field placement require? An astute sense of the game and of space. All the above games require an instinctive awareness and utilization of space. While doing crosswords, we need to see length of the words we fill in, the matching of the common letters, and so on. What about board games like chess? While playing, you need to think of a winning strategy. For this you need to construct the possible movement at any instant, giving the conditions under which the different pieces are allowed to move. In Ludo, Chaupad, Trade, and other such games, the players use a lot of mathematics.

Even nature embraces mathematics completely. We see so much of symmetry around us and have a deep sense of awareness and appreciation of patterns. Observe any natural thing and find out symmetry or pattern in it. Change of day into night, summer into winter etc. In plants there are innumerable examples of symmetry, shapes, patterns, etc. Such examples exist in animals, in objects, in pictures and other things as well. The sun rises and sets at specified moments. The stars appear at fixed time. Mathematics runs in the veins of natural sciences like Physics and Astronomy. This subject is inextricably incorporated with world and the natural phenomena. Galileo defined, 'mathematics as a language in which God has written the world'.

We also use the concept of probability so many times in casual conversation. For example, the Intercity train is late many times. It would be late today also! There is no possibility of rain today. Or he would certainly come; he always keeps his word.

Thus we can say that there is no science, no art and no profession, where mathematics is not used. The accuracy and exactness of a science is determined to a major extent by the amount of mathematics utilized in it. Mathematics is developed according to the necessity. When man first wanted to answer the question ask, how many? how much? and how long?, he invented arithmetic. He devised algebra to simplify arithmetical problems. For measurement, he invented geometry. To find the position of high mountains and stars, trigonometry was invented. The most salient feature of nature phenomena is change, for which the most important branch of mathematics known as calculus was invented to measure change. To measure social phenomena, humans invented statistics. Mathematical knowledge is thus indispensable and no one can hope to advance ahead as an investigator in most of the exact sciences, if he or she has no mathematical knowledge. Therefore arithmetic is the language of commercial activity, algebra gives the idea of functional dependence and generalization, and geometry teaches logical thinking and natural design. All these combine together to produce a very valuable literature of interpretation, control and progress. We understand the world better. Graphical representation of numbers is becoming very common. Mathematics in home decoration designs, measurement and construction, in banking and business, in protection of life and property, in painting and art is playing a vital role.

To conclude we can say, mathematics is all around us. It permeates all those areas of our life that interest and excite us. May be we are not aware of it. An activity or an incidence or phenomenon can be looked upon and studied from several angles. If we look for mathematics in it, we will find it. Once we have our mathematical eyes open and we start noticing rules and patterns, we can see mathematics in almost everything—a song, a story book, a cup of coffee, the path taken by a fly while buzzing around, the shape of a match-box and the number of its surfaces, the proportion of paper required to cover these surfaces, electric wiring in your home, pattern in leaves, and so on. Everywhere we have mathematics. But what is mathematics? How can we define it? Let us see

1.3 Definitions of Mathematics

The dictionary meaning of mathematics is, 'Mathematics is the science of numbers and space' or 'Mathematics is the science of measurement, quantity and magnitude'.

According to the New English Dictionary, "Mathematics —in a strict sense—is an abstract science which investigates deductively the conclusion implement in the elementary conception of spatial and numerical relations."

According to the Britannica Junior Encyclopedia, "Mathematics is the science of numbers. It covers, among other things, their operations and relations. Mathematics is also the science of shapes: how they are "put together" and measured.

According to the Britannica Concise Encyclopedia, "Mathematics is the science of structure, order and relation that has evolved from counting, measuring and describing the shapes of objects. It deals with logical reasoning and quantities calculations".

According to Angels," Mathematics is a science whose subject matter is special forms and quantitative relationships of the real world".

According to A.N. Whitehead," Mathematics in its widest significance is the development of all types of formal deductive reasoning".

According to Pierce," Mathematics is the science, which draws necessary conclusion".

According to Locke," Mathematic is a way to settle in the mind of children a habit of reasoning".

1.4 Interpretations of the term Mathematics

The term mathematics has been interpreted and explained in various ways:

- Mathematics is the science dealing with amounts, sizes and shapes, as explained by numbers and signs. (blog.hienglish.com/faye 1982/articles/18216.html.)
- Mathematics is the science that deals with numbers, quantities, shapes, patterns, measurement, and the concepts related to them. And their relationships include arithmetic, algebra, geometry, trigonometry, calculus, etc.
- Mathematics is the investigation of axiomatically defined abstract structures using symbolic logic and mathematical notation. It is commonly defined as the study of patterns of structure, change, and space; even more informally, one might say it is the study of "figures and numbers". Because it is not empirical, it is not a science.(Wikipedia.org/wiki/ Mathematics)
- Mathematics is a kind of language with its own vocabulary and grammar. This vocabulary consists of concepts, terms, facts, assumptions, symbols etc. while the syntax relates to the principles, processes, functional relationship and the like.
- Mathematics is no more than counting, which gets complex with various means, or shortcuts for counting. Division is counting, using groups. In other words, how many, whatever in groups of two can be counted in a body of four—two. Algebra is counting by doing the same to both sides of an equation, keeping the equation in balance by adding, subtracting, multiplying or dividing one side of the equation exactly by doing what you did to the other side. In Algebra the 'x' or 'y' do not represent numbers; they merely represent whatever is being counted. They remain unchanged. They are qualitative.
- Mathematicians often represent things with abstract ideas, such as numbers or perfectly straight lines, and then work

with those ideas alone. The "things" from which they abstract can be ideas themselves (for example, a proposition about "all equal-sided triangles" or "all odd numbers").

To conclude, mathematics can be defined as: Mathematics is the study of quantity, structure, space and change. It has historically developed through the use of abstraction and logical reasoning, from counting, calculation, measurement, and the study of the shapes and motions of physical objects. In a simple way we can say that mathematic has originated from numbers and number system is its special field, from which other branches of mathematics are developed. It is a systematized, organized and an exact branch of science.

Mathematics is also used to refer to the insight gained by mathematicians by doing mathematics, also known as the body of mathematical knowledge. The latter meaning of mathematics includes the mathematics used to do calculations and is an indispensable tool in the natural sciences, engineering and social sciences.

Thus, we have seen what is mathematics and how much important it is for us. In the next chapter we will discuss about the importance of teaching of mathematics.

2

Importance of Teaching Mathematics

2.1 Introduction

Education is the process of all round development of human beings. The development should bring about both qualitative and quantitative behavioural changes in individual in a desired direction. The development and changes occur gradually over a period of time. The outcomes of these changes are in the form of acquisition of knowledge, development of understanding about different phenomena related to life, inculcation of good human values, creation of interest and attitude and ability to perform certain skills. Ultimately, these developments in scientific and technological, social and economical, ethical and cultural areas enable the individual to think logically and rationally for leading a happy, purposeful and socially productive life. Sometimes, we speak of educational goals, which are general statements about expectations in terms of attainments at the end of a course or stage in a school or in a college. The goals originate from many sources, primary being the requirement of individuals, society and the nation. Goals provide directions for defining and developing the system. Goals further comprise of a number of aims and aims comprise of a number of objectives. The objectives can be further stated in terms of a number of specific objectives (also called specifications). Therefore, objectives need to be viewed in relation to aims and goals of the education system. Specific objectives in behavioural terms are both measurable and observable. These need to be stated in terms of pupil's behaviour rather than teachers behaviour.

2.2 Objectives of Teaching Mathematics

2.2.1 *At Primary Level*

There is a need to give stress on some special objectives at primary level. We have to create some new objectives, which are as follows:

1. Solve the problems related to his daily life and environment.
2. Start attaining higher levels of education by understanding the basic concepts.
3. Develop an interest in mathematics so that he gets ready to study it by keen efforts.
4. Learn about the different topics of mathematics to make his knowledge reasonably vast.
5. Get a chance to enter the world of mathematics with pleasure.
6. Develop a relationship with mathematics.
7. Understand mathematics as a concrete subject.
8. Prepare himself for undertaking higher knowledge of mathematics.
9. Learn to calculate quickly with clarity.
10. Recognize symbols and signs of mathematics and uses them to solve problems easily in day-to-day life.

2.2.2 *At Secondary Level*

1. Solve problems of daily life pertaining to various occupations and environment related to mathematics.
2. Become capable of clarifying high concepts of mathematics and start clarifying the knowledge pertaining to it.
3. Develop a stable interest towards mathematics.
4. Develop reasoning ability and logical thinking with the help of mathematics.
5. Gain and attain abstract knowledge on the basis of concrete knowledge of mathematics.
6. Attain mathematical knowledge used in various professions and subjects.
7. Understand the mathematical concepts.
8. Start getting the feeling of mathematical discipline.
9. Find mathematics interesting and enjoy it.

10. Start knowing about the importance of mathematics in Sanskrit.

2.3 Instructional Objectives according to NCERT

2.3.1 Primary Stage

1. *Knowledge Objective*: The student acquires the knowledge of numbers, figures, geometrical shapes etc.
   Specifications: To show the achievement of this objective, the student:
   - 1.1 recalls number and basic operation of numbers, units of measurement etc.
   - 1.2 recognises shapes, figures, numbers etc.
2. *Understanding Objective*: The student develops understanding of fundamental operations and solves problems using these operation.
   Specifications: To demonstrate the achievements of this objective, the student:
   - 2.1 counts, reads and writes numbers.
   - 2.2 uses vocabulary related to numbers.
   - 2.3 adds, subtracts, multiply and divides numbers orally and in the written form.
   - 2.4 arranges the numbers in sequence.
   - 2.5 solves problems stated in numbers, fractions and decimals using basic numerical operation.
   - 2.6 reads and interprets temperature, chart, tables etc.
3. *Application Objectives*: The students apply knowledge and understanding to solve mathematical problems.
   Specification: To show the achievements of this objective, the student:
   - 3.1 calculates length, area and volume of geometrical figures.
   - 3.2 calculates days, months and dates using a calendar.
   - 3.3 reads school, bus and railways timetable.
   - 3.4 handles simple money transactions.
   - 3.5 analyses problems systematically.

4. *Computational Objectives:* The student acquires computational and drawing skills.
   Specifications: To demonstrate the achievement of this objective, the student:
   4.1 draws geometrical shapes and figures.
   4.2 identifies and draws two dimensional shapes.
   4.3 interprets meaningfully, information depicted through pictures, charts, graphs from newspapers and magazines etc.
5. *Thinking Objective:* the student develops thinking and reasoning power.
   Specifications: To show the achievement of this objective, the student:
   5.1 asks thoughtful questions/problems.
   5.2 reasons deductively and inductively.
   5.3 observes keenly.
   5.4 solves logically.
6. *Interest and Attitude Objective:* the student displays interest and attitude in mathematics.
   Specifications: To display these attributes the student:
   6.1 solves mathematical puzzles, riddles etc.
   6.2 designs mathematical models, games etc.
   6.3 plays number games.
   6.4 generalizes patterns.

2.3.2 *Secondary Stage*

1. *Knowledge Objective:* To acquire the knowledge of terms, facts, concepts, symbols, definitions, principles and formulae of mathematics.
   Specifications: To demonstrate the achievement of the above objective, the pupil:
   1.1 recalls and reproduces, terms, facts, definitions, formulae, concepts, processes etc.
   1.2 recognizes formulae, figures, concepts, procedures and processes etc.

2. *Comprehension Objective:* To develop the understanding of the concepts, principles and processes of mathematics.
   Specifications: To demonstrate the achievement of the above objective, the pupil:
   - 2.1 gives illustration.
   - 2.2 detects errors in a statement, formulae or figure and corrects them.
   - 2.3 explains concepts, principles, configuration etc.
   - 2.4 discriminates between closely related concepts, principles etc.
   - 2.5 classifies as per given criteria.
   - 2.6 identifies relationship among the given data.
   - 2.7 translates variable statement into symbolic relationship and *vice versa*.
   - 2.8 estimates the results.
   - 2.9 reads and interprets the given charts, graphs and data.
   - 2.10 verifies properties, indicates hypothesis.
   - 2.11 solves numerical problems.
   - 2.12 uses calculator and computer.
3. *Applications Objectives:* To apply the acquired knowledge and understanding of mathematics in unfamiliar situations or new problems.
   Specifications: To demonstrate the achievement of above the objective, the pupil:
   - 3.1 analysis and solves problems.
   - 3.2 finds out the adequacy or relevance of data.
   - 3.3 establishes relationship among the given data.
   - 3.4 selects the appropriate method for solving the method.
   - 3.5 suggests alternative method.
4. *Skill Objectives*: To acquire different skills like, (a) Computing (b) Drawing geometrical figures and grapes, and (c) Reading tables, charts, graphs etc.
   Specifications: To demonstrate the achievement of the above objective, the pupil:
   - 4.1 carries out oral calculations with ease and speed.
   - 4.2 does written calculations with ease and speed.
   - 4.3 handles geometrical instruments with ease and proficiency.

4.4 measures accurately.
4.5 draws free hand diagrams with ease.
4.6 draws figures accurately.
4.7 draws figures according to scale.
4.8 reads data—table, with speed and accuracy.
4.9 performs experiment in mathematics laboratory comfortably.

5. *Appreciation Objective:* To appreciate the use of mathematics in day-to-day life.
Specifications: To demonstrate the achievement of the above objective, the pupil:

5.1 appreciates the use of mathematics in other branches of science.
5.2 appreciates the symmetry of figures and patterns.
5.3 appreciates qualities like brevity and exactness through the study of mathematics.
5.4 appreciates the contribution of mathematicians in general and Indians mathematicians in particular.

6. *Intent Objective:* To develop interest in mathematics.
Specifications: To demonstrate the achievement of the above objective, the pupil:

6.1 solves mathematical puzzles.
6.2 participates in the activities of Mathematics club.
6.3 finds short cuts for solving the problems.
6.4 reads additional material in mathematics.
6.5 puts additional problems to the teacher.

7. *Attitude Objective:* To develop scientific attitude through the study of mathematics.
Specifications: To demonstrate the achievement of the above objective, the pupil:

7.1 accepts a proposition only when logically proved.
7.2 examines all the aspects of a problem.
7.3 points out errors boldly if convinced.
7.4 accepts errors without hesitation.
7.5 respects the opinion of others.
7.6 keeps an open mind and develops the habit of logical thinking.

Thus, we have seen what mathematics is, and why it should be taught *i.e.*, its importance in our life. Due to its unique role in solving everyday problems, it has occupied a significant position in school curriculum. Necessity of teaching more mathematics and better mathematics has emerged from the advancement of this subject itself and its applications in other disciplines. In the next chapters we will see how we can teach it in a better way *i.e.* in a simple and interesting manner.

3

Ways of Teaching Mathematics

3.1 Introduction

According to 'The National Focus Group on The Teaching of Mathematics', the main aim of mathematics education in schools is, 'the mathematization of the child's thought processes.' In the words of Dravid Wheeler, it is "more useful to know how to mathematize than to know a lot of mathematics".

3.2 How to Achieve the Main Aim?

To achieve this aim, there is a need to develop the inner resources of the growing child. In developing a child's inner resources, the role that mathematics plays is mostly about thinking. Since mathematics helps in training and disciplining the mind as also developing the power of thinking and reasoning. It is a mental tool for the training and exercise of intellectual functions. Besides being an independent subject of study, it has its applications in other branches of knowledge. Mathematical skills and their applications form an indispensable tool in our daily life.

In spite of all these characteristics, mathematics is considered as a very dull and difficult subject due to the hierarchy of concepts and largely deductive and abstract nature of the subject. A phobia has been created in the minds of children that mathematics is tough to learn. As a result, most of the students are not taking interest in the subject and it has become one of the main causes of students' failure in mathematics. No doubt, mathematics is an inter-connected series of concepts and conceptual schemes and a student who can concentrate well can learn well. Thus, clarity of thought and pursuing assumptions to logical conclusions is central to the mathematical enterprise. There are many ways of thinking, and the kind of thinking one learns in mathematics is an ability to handle abstractions. Even more importantly, what mathematics offers is a way of doing things: to handle and be able to solve mathematical problems, and more generally, to have the right attitude for problem solving and to be able to attack all kinds of problems in a systematic manner. An important consequence of such requirements is that school mathematics must be *activity-oriented.*

My experience of mathematics teaching shows that students take part in the learning process. They investigate and explore, and thereby can actually 'find' mathematics themselves. Great mathematicians in times past and now, do just that: they experiment and try this and that, make guesses and test them. With some guidance and with today's great learning aids a child can 're-discover' mathematical truths in reasonable time (of course it many times took those mathematicians a great deal of time). Students should be made to THINK, instead of being provided with readymade answers to thought provoking questions.

Rules are not just being given like "Here it is, now believe it and use it in these 50 problems". Try to give the understanding of derivation of the rules, background and their reasons-somehow the rule is "proven" or justified. The explanation might be totally different depending on grade. For example, to a third grader you may explain, "You can't divide by zero because seven bananas divided between zero people just doesn't make sense. You can't ask how many does each one get since there is no one to get any." To a eighth grader you can present the argument that "Well, if 3/0 = 1, say, then we get the multiplication fact 1 × 0 = 3, which is not possible. Or if you try 3/0 = 0, then you should get 0 × 0 = 3, which doesn't work." Then, in high school or in college they might encounter that 3/0 = 1. The argument given may vary according to the level. All this can (and should) start as early as possible, and continue on!

Many children love mathematics in the beginning, but something during the school years kills that joy. Certainly we do need to teach the students the above mentioned rules but simultaneously we also need to practice and drill with them, these rules. There is a need to strike a balance between teaching and practice of mathematics.

Teaching of mathematics has been a challenge to the teachers since the origin of human race. In most schools mathematics is taught as a mere "Here are the rules, memorize them, we'll drill them for the rest of the lesson." That does not promote conceptual understanding nor dose it tie the concepts together. The memorized, non-understood procedures can quickly faint from the memory. What students learn is often very shallow and doesn't give them understanding of the actual concepts and thereby doesn't provide adequate background for higher education studies. An international review of 8th-grade classes suggests, "Teachers must do more to help students understand the concepts of mathematics, not just the mechanics of how to solve an arithmetic, algebra or geometry problem".

According to 'The National Focus Group on The Teaching of Mathematics' school mathematics takes place in a situation where:

- *Children learn to enjoy mathematics*: This is an important goal, based on the premise that mathematics can be both used and enjoyed life-long, and that school is the best place for creating such a taste for mathematics. On the other hand, creating (or not removing) a fear of mathematics can deprive children of an important faculty for life.
- *Children see mathematics as something to talk about, to communicate*: To discuss among themselves, to work together on. Making mathematics a part of children's life experiences is the best possible way of mathematics education.
- *Children use abstractions to perceive relationships, to see structure, to reason about things, to argue the truth or falsity of statements*: Logical thinking is a great gift mathematics can offer us and inculcating such habits of thinking and communication in children is a principle of teaching mathematics.

Thus, teachers expect to engage every child in class and try different methods to develop a solid foundation in mathematical concepts. They can try to teach mathematics in such a way that mathematics becomes a good, interesting and real subject, which is related to their daily life thus creating a keen interest and desire in children to study mathematics. It is observed that students are active by nature; they enjoy looking and feeling the new objects. When they have interest in any material, they try to collect complete information about it and the method of using it. It is seen very often that only those things are remembered or permanently stored in mind, which have influenced the mind highly. If everything is made clear and understandable to the students then this makes it easier to memorize the concept by developing the real image in mind. It is also necessary to motivate the children by arousing and maintaining their interest in mathematics, to remove the mathematics' phobia. This will create in them a positive attitude towards the subject.

According to Improving Student Achievement in Mathematics Part 1: Research findings, the following teaching methods have been shown to consistently improve student performance in mathematics:

- The extent of the opportunity to learn mathematics.
- Teaching for meaning.
- Learning both concepts and skills by solving problems.
- Opportunity to discover and invent new knowledge, and practice what one has learned.
- Incorporating students' intuitive solution methods into teaching, especially if there is students' interaction and discussion.
- Using small groups of students to work on activities and problems.
- Whole-class discussion following individual and group work.
- Emphasizing number sense in teaching.
- Long-term use of *concrete materials or manipulative.*

It is a fact that there are so many abstractions, that cannot be followed easily by the students. To make such abstracts or complex ideas less abstract, rather concrete, teachers can give something concrete into the hands of the students, which will give a better picture. This concrete material is simply termed as *teaching aid*.

There is a popular Chinese saying that:

"The things, which I hear, I may forget.
The things, which I see, I may remember.
The things, which I do, I can not forget".

In the next chapter we will discuss what is teaching aid and why we should use it?

4

Teaching Aids in Mathematics

4.1 Introduction

Indian Education Commission, 1964-66, emphasis on the use of teaching aids by saying: "In order to raise the level of education in schools, teaching aids are very necessary. No doubt, it can bring revolution in the field of education."

4.2 What is a Teaching Aid?

We can define teaching aid as, any device, method or experience used for facilitating teaching learning purpose, including text books, supplementary reading material, audio-visuals, and other sensory material of abstract concepts are actually, aids to imagination of pupils.

4.3 Why We should Use Teaching Aids?

Teaching aids are helpful tools for teaching a concept. Teachers can use them to:

- help learners to improve different skills,
- illustrate or reinforce a fact, idea or skill, and
- relieve anxiety, fears, or boredom, since many teaching aids are like games.

It is a known fact that the knowledge obtained through the five senses of a human being is more stable. As much and as many senses are used to gain new experiences, the concepts become more and more easy, since most of the learning in children takes place at the sensory level. According to Weber "Senses are the gateways of learning."

The modern educationists also believe that the knowledge which is gained by the use of more senses becomes clearer, stable and useful. In this context teaching aids are essential for effective teaching. They influence the minds of learners through their senses. They are necessary to make the lesson more interesting, meaningful and useful. According to Albrecht Durer, "It is easier to believe what you see than what you hear; but if you see and hear both, you can understand readily and retain more lastingly."

Teaching aids are especially useful for elementary classes because students of that age do not have high perfection and maturity level. They cannot think abstractly like us. Famous educationist Piaget has proved through his experiments that students must be active in the class and activeness can be created with the help of tools. The success of teaching methods depends upon the appropriate use of teaching aids. The difficult principles or concepts of lesson that are new can be made clear with the use of concrete objects. It is a psychological fact that with the help of concrete things an abstract figure of a concept is formed in the minds of children by which the child can easily understand even minute things.

Hence, the traditional approach of teaching mathematics in which abstract concepts are usually presented to the students in an authoritarian verbal way should be discouraged and activity approach, which stresses the presentation of concrete experiences, should be encouraged. Thus, mathematics has to be learned by doing rather than reading or listening. These 'doings' of mathematics give rise to the need of teaching aids.

4.4 Teaching Aids for Mathematics Teaching

Mathematics is an abstract subject and the learning of abstract concepts becomes extremely difficult if the students have to learn them through verbal explanation presented by the teacher. The learning can be made easier and effective if the teaching is supplemented with the use of teaching aids. While teaching abstract mathematical concepts, visualization using concrete objects and the use of the multi-sensory experiences facilitate understanding of the concepts. The use of teaching aids help the teaching and learning of mathematics in the following ways:

- Mathematics is such a subject in which the use of teaching aids is very helpful in clarifying the abstract ideas, concepts, facts, principles and rules *i.e.* they help in clear understanding of the subject.
- By the use of teaching aids mathematics becomes easy, good, interactive and real subject, which is related to their daily life. They are the best motivators. The students work with more interest.
- Teaching aids stimulate pupil participation. They are based on the principle of 'learning by doing' and hence it follows the basic teaching principle like 'simple to complex', 'known to unknown', 'concrete to abstract' etc.
- Teaching aids help to impart permanent knowledge. They help in creating a lasting impression on the mind of the learner. Things are well retained in the mind since the sensory impressions are more permanent.
- Teaching aids help in saving time and energy because it takes a long time to clarify an abstract idea just verbally but if some concepts are explained not only by words but also by using teaching aids then the point can be made clear at once and it saves both time and labour.
- Teaching aids helps to meet the needs of individual students. All students of the same class do not gain knowledge in the same way. Some people learn by listening, some by looking, some by looking and hearing both, but a majority of them learn by doing. They feel comfortable in obtaining knowledge with the use of various kinds of teaching aids.

To summarize we can say that, teaching aids lead the pupil to discover mathematical facts. It is based on the principle of 'learning by doing', 'learning by observation' and proceeding from concrete to abstract. This is nothing but an extension to a more elaborated and practical form of Inductive Method. The principles have to be discovered, generalized and established. If properly used, they help in removal of abstract nature of mathematics. Thus, they make the subject interesting as it combines play and activity, and it results in better learning and long retention of concepts.

4.5 Principles for the Use of Teaching Aids

You may be able to buy some teaching aids. More likely, however, you will need to make them. Making them will give you the opportunity to use locally available materials and to provide exactly the kinds of teaching aids that will benefit the learners. It will also give you the opportunity to involve the local people in creating them.

Follow these steps to use teaching aids:

- The selection of teaching aids should suit the age-level, grade-level, intelligence-level and the experience of the students.
- The teaching aids should be selected according to the general interests and abilities of the pupils.
- They should be true representatives of the real things. They should be accurate, truthful and realistic.
- Find or make suitable teaching aids.
- As far as possible, low cost, easily and locally available material should be used in the preparation of a teaching aid *i.e.* they should be cheep and easily available.
- The size of the aid should be neither too large nor too small. It should be clearly visible to the students.
- The teaching aid should be displayed properly so that all the students are able to see it, observe it, and derive maximum benefits out of it.
- Experiment and practice with them beforehand so that you know how to use them.
- Teaching aids should be used only at the right moment. Remember to use them whenever they are appropriate. If it is meant for introduction of the lesson, it should be shown at the that time. If a number of aids are to be used then every aid must be used at the appropriate time and not in a haphazard manner. The systematic display gives good results.
- Teaching aid should serve some purpose *i.e.* it should have specific educational value, besides being interesting and motivating. The aid should be kept before the students as long as it serves some purpose. It should be removed when the purpose has been fulfilled.

- Teaching aids should be according to the local needs of the students.
- They should be tested and revised if necessary.

Thus, for the effective use of teaching aids we should follow these steps. Beside this we have seen that what are teaching aids and why should we use them especially in mathematics teaching. In the next chapter we will discuss different types of teaching aids.

5

Types of Teaching Aids

5.1 Introduction

We can divide the teaching aids into two categories:

5.1.1 Traditional teaching aids.
5.1.2 Modern teaching aids.

5.1.1 Traditional Teaching Aids

Traditionally we use textbooks and black board for teaching of mathematics.

Textbook is an essential and important teaching aid for teaching and learning of any subject. In a text book, the subject matter is organized and collected at a single place. The textbook provides directions to teachers and students about how much content has to be covered in a particular class. Students also get their class work as well as homework from the textbook. At the end, examination or evaluation of a student is done on the basis of the contents given in the textbook.

Black board is the most important visual aid for teaching mathematics. It is the most indispensable tool in the hands of mathematics teacher, therefore mathematics cannot be taught effectively without the use of it. Use of colour chalks can make the black board work appealing and attractive. A mathematics teacher can make use of the black board:

- To develop various steps of the solution of a problem or proof of a theorem.
- For drawing important diagrams.
- To write down certain important points on the blackboard to focus the attention of the students on those points.

- To plot certain graphs.
- For writing down the problem for drill and homework assignment.
- Summarize the day's lesson.

With the help of textbook and black board, teachers can cover the syllabus. But, as it is discussed earlier, mathematics is a difficult subject due to its structure, and at the same time it is a subject, which is widely used in all walks of life. Therefore, only completing the prescribed syllabus is not sufficient. Rather, for a better advancement of the society it is our duty, that as mathematics teachers, we should teach the students in such a manner that along with the conceptual learning mathematical attitude, logical thinking is also developed. The students should be able to use logic not only in solving the mathematical problems in the classroom or given in the text but also the problems they face in their daily lives.

To serve this purpose, the first and foremost step should be, to change our method of teaching, *i.e.* from traditional to modern methods. Mathematics is a subject, which has to be learnt by doing rather than by reading or listening. The students should take part in the learning process. They should be able to investigate and explore, and thereby actually 'find' mathematics themselves. This doing of mathematics, gives rise to the need of a suitable method and a suitable supporting material. Thus, the type of supporting material needs to include modern teaching aids with the traditional ones, since old ones are necessary but not sufficient. For carrying out such type of teaching of mathematics Modern Teaching Aids should be used.

5.1.2 Modern Teaching Aids

Various types of teaching aids used in mathematics are:

(i) Real Objects
(ii) Charts
(iii) Models
(iv) Use of paper

  (a) Paper folding
  (b) Paper cutting and pasting

(v) Flannel Board
(vi) Bulletin Board.
(vii) Projective aids such as Magic lanterns, filmstrip projector, Epidiascope motion picture, Radio, T.V. and Computer etc.
(viii) Excursions etc.

Thus, we have various types of teaching aids. Here, in the next chapters, we will discuss only the first four types in details and the rest will be discussed briefly.

6

Real Objects

6.1 Introduction

Real objects are the most useful and most effective means of providing direct experience to the pupil. We can use coins, pebbles, marbles, pens, pencils, sticks, seeds, balls, flowers, fruits, etc .to teach the concept of counting, addition, subtraction, multiplication, division, average, percentage, profit & loss etc. Concept of the shape of rectangle and its area can be easily taught with the help of black board, wall of the room, top of the table, play ground, etc. Similarly the shape of square can be taught with the help of carrum board, chessboard or lodu board etc.

We can also use students as an object to give different concepts. For example counting, addition and subtraction of numbers can be taught easily by taking different number of students. Concept of angles can be easily introduced with the help of students by performing the following activity:

- Ask students to stand in a straight line. In this line mark a student as *Center* by giving him a flag or a card. Now ask the students of any one side of the centre to move but in a straight line while the students of the other side of the center will not move. Tell them that the student acting as the center is the *Vertex* of the angle and the two lines of students, one on each side of the vertex are the two *Arms* or *Sides* of the angle, where the line of students which are not moving is the *Base line* of the angle. In this way they can get the idea of Angle, Vertex and Base line. And also they can make different types of angle easily.

Some of the concepts that can be developed through the use of real objects are:

6.2 Concept of Numbers

Rule: The quantity of the object represents the number

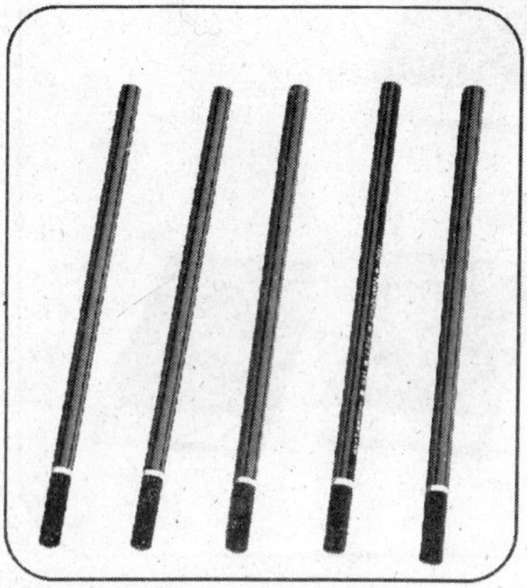

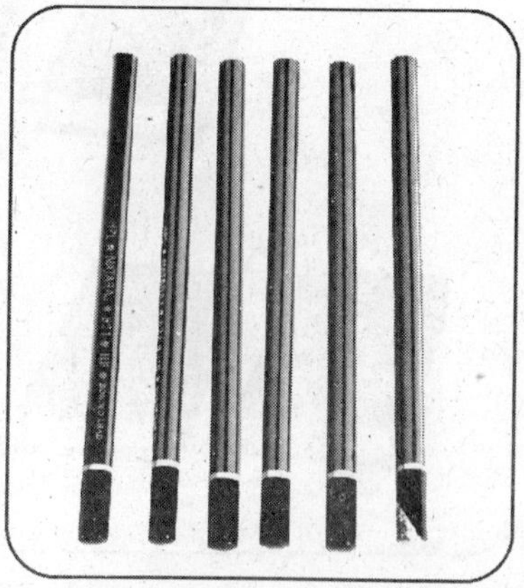

Activity

(i) *Material Required*: Pens, pencils, pebbles, flowers etc.
(ii) *Description of the Activity:*

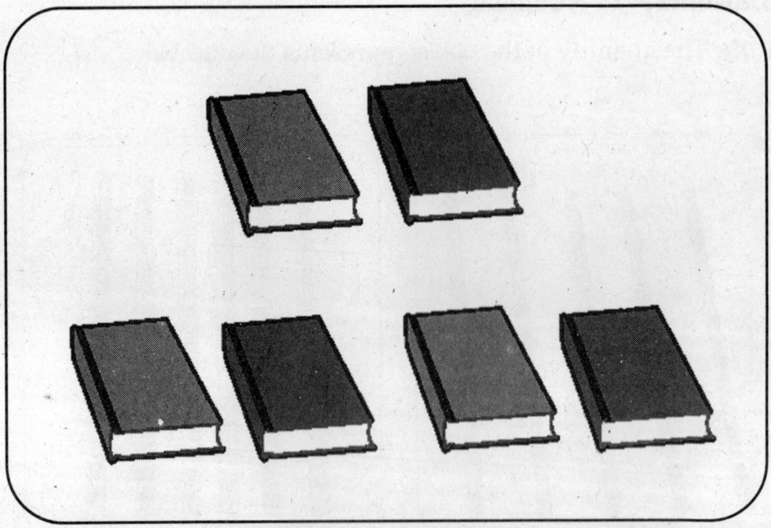

If a teacher wants to teach the concept of numbers with the help of real objects like pens, pencils, pebbles, books, flowers etc., he/she should follow the following three steps:

1. Introduction with object *i.e.* teacher should introduce the object (books or pencils) to the students.
2. Talk about the quantity of object: *i.e.*, after introduction, teacher should talk about the quantity of the object.
3. Talk about numeral *i.e.* after discussing the quantity, the teacher should introduce the concept of numerals.

In this process, this point should be clear to students, that the quantity of the object represents the number, any other property like size, colour or arrangement etc. are not important at this stage. For example the teacher can explain that the number 6 represents the quantity and not any other quality like size or arrangement. Generally students think the bigger or dark coloured things represent more quantity than the smaller or the light coloured things.

6.3 Concept of Currency

Rule: Values of different coins and notes, their addition and subtraction.

Activity

(i) *Material Required*: Coins and notes of different values.
(ii) *Description of the Activity:*

With the help of real coins and notes a teacher can easily give the concept of currency, its addition, subtraction, multiplication and division.

For example following game can be played to give the concept of addition subtractions multiplicity and division of money.

Ask two or three students to pretend as they are the shopkeeper. Give some books, notebooks, pens, pencils, eraser, sharpener etc (from the class) and ask them to give the rate for each thing. Distribute some notes (game notes) to other students and ask them to buy these things. In playing this game, they learn the operations of money and also to estimate how many things they can buy from their money.

6.4 Concept of Time

Rule: Concept of time.

Activity

(i) *Material Required*: Real clock.

(ii) *Description of the Activity*:

Real clock or a model of clock can be used to teach the concept of time.

After showing a watch, discuss it with students about numbers, written on it, its different hands and their functions. Also discuss with them, why are there precisely 12 hours time in a watch and not 10, 11, 13, 14 etc.

6.5 Concept of Average

Rule: Average = $\dfrac{\text{Sum of number}}{\text{Number of addends}}$

Activity

(i) *Material Required*: Toy cars or Pencils.
(ii) *Description of the Activity*:

Real object can also be used to give the concept of average, *e.g.* a teacher can give 3 cars to a student, 5 cars to another student and 10 cars to the third student and ask them to divide these cars equally among themselves. The students divide the cars amongst them and each of them gets 6 cars.

This activity can be repeated by distributing different number of cars or pencils each time. After this, the teacher can explains that this equal number, which you get, is known as *Average* in mathematical language. This can be calculated as:

$$\text{Average} = \frac{\text{Sum of cars}}{\text{Number of students}}$$

Thus,

$$\text{Average} = \frac{\text{Sum of number}}{\text{Number of addends}}$$

6.6 Point, Line Segment, Line, and Ray

Rule

- *Point*: A small dot made by sharp pencil can give the concept of point. A point determines a location.
- *Line Segment*: Shortest distance between two points can give the concept of line segment. These two points are called the end points of the line segment. Line segment may be defined as collection of points in straight line.
- *A Line*: A line extends indefinitely in both the directions so it contains a countless number of points.
- *Ray*: A ray is a portion of line. It starts at one point and goes endlessly in a direction.

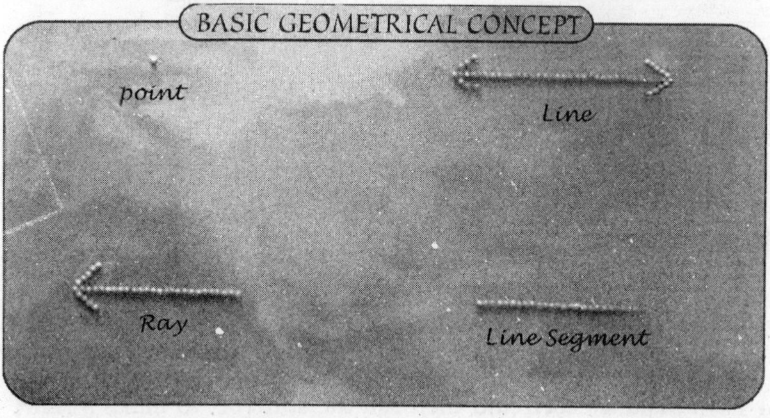

Activity

(i) *Material Required*: Beads.
(ii) *Description of the activity*:

Teacher can give the concept of point, line, line segment and ray with the help of beads by making the above model. In this model one bead is used to portray the concept of a point. Concept of line segment, line and ray are also portrayed with the help of beads since line segment, line or ray is a collection of points in a straight path.

6.7 Pythagoras Theorem

Rule : $(\text{Hypotenuse})^2 = (\text{Perpendicular})^2 + (\text{Base})^2$

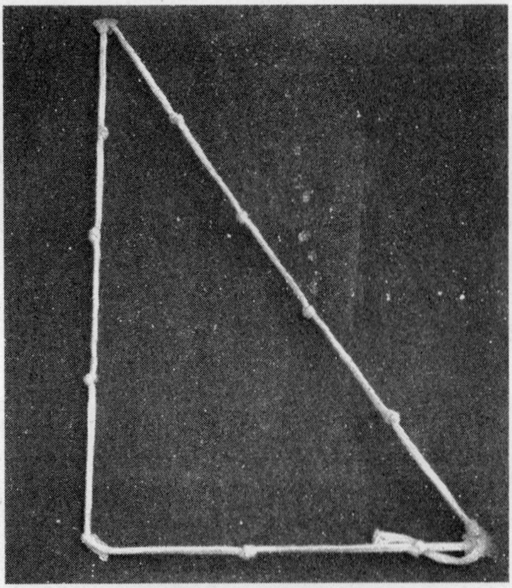

Activity

(i) *Material Required*: Rope or thread.
(ii) *Description of the Activity*:

For this the teacher can take a rope or thread and make 12 knots at 1 cm distance each and then ask the students to make a right angled triangle with the help of this rope. Students try this and when the right angled triangle is complete they find that the lengths of different sides contains 3, 4 and 5 knots i.e. their lengths are 3, 4 and 5 cm. This activity can be repeated by making 24, 36 and so on equidistant knots. After making the right triangles and counting the knots in each side they get the relationship.

$$(\text{Hypotenuse})^2 = (\text{Perpendicular})^2 + (\text{Base})^2$$

This is the required Pythagoras theorem.

6.8 Concept of π

Rule: The value of π = 22/7

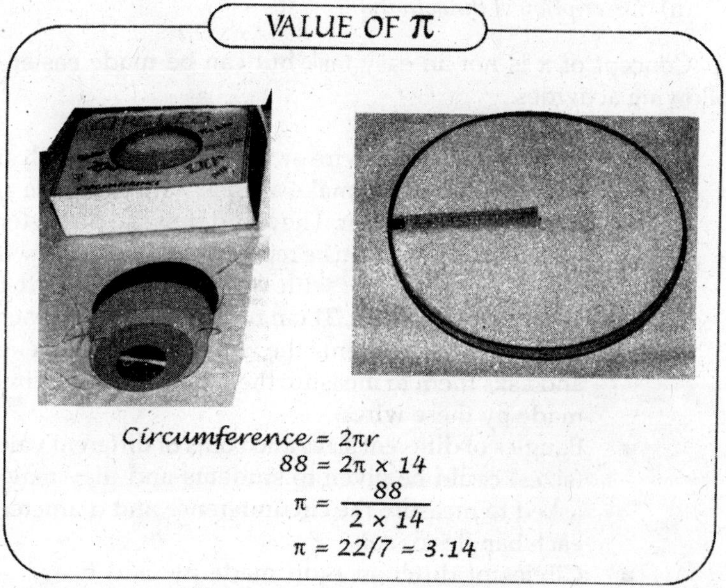

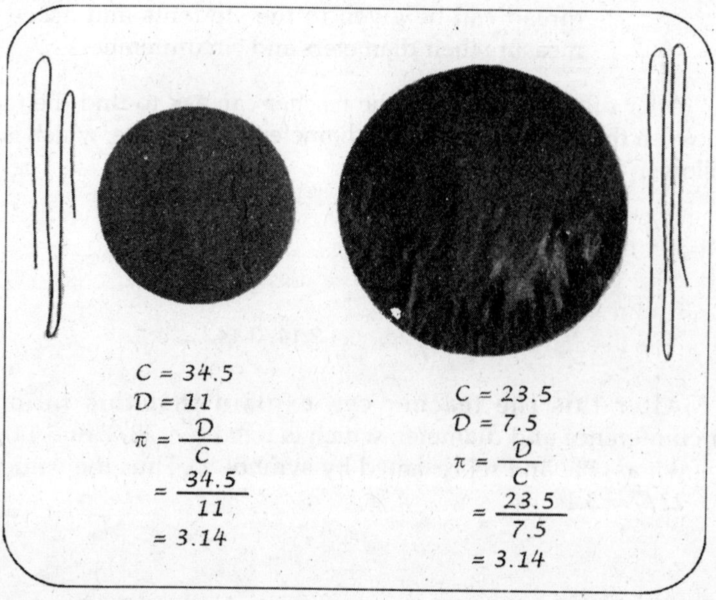

Activity

(i) *Material Required*: Wire, Bangles, Coins, Card board, Thread, Inch tape.

(ii) *Description of the activity*:

Concept of π is not an easy task but can be made easier by following activities:

- Teacher can take a wire or wool of 22 cm length and ask the students to make a circle with this wire and measure its diameter. They find that the diameter is 7 cm. This activity can be repeated by taking the wires of 44 cm, 66 cm etc. with which they find that the diameters are 14 cm, 21 cm respectively. The teacher then gives the students the wires of different length and asks them to measure the diameter of the circles made by these wires.
- Bangles of different sizes and coins of different values (sizes) could be given to students and they may be asked to measure the circumference and diameter of each bangles or coin.
- Circles of different radii made by card board and thread can be given to the students and asked to measure their diameters and circumferences.

After different activities the teacher can ask to find the ratio between the circumference and diameter in each case, which is as follows:

$$\frac{22}{7}, \frac{44}{14}, \frac{66}{21}, \frac{88}{28}, \frac{110}{35}, \frac{132}{42} \ldots\ldots\ldots, \frac{34.5}{11}, \frac{23.5}{7.5}, \ldots\ldots\ldots$$

$$\frac{22}{7}, \frac{22}{7}, \frac{22}{7} \ldots\ldots\ldots, 3.14, 3.14, \ldots\ldots\ldots$$

After this the teacher can explain that this ratio of circumference and diameter, which is fixed (*i.e.* 22/7 or 3.14), is known as Pie and represented by symbol, π. Thus the value of π = 22/7 = 3.14.

6.9 Volume of Cylinder

Rule: Volume of Cylinder = $\pi r^2 h$

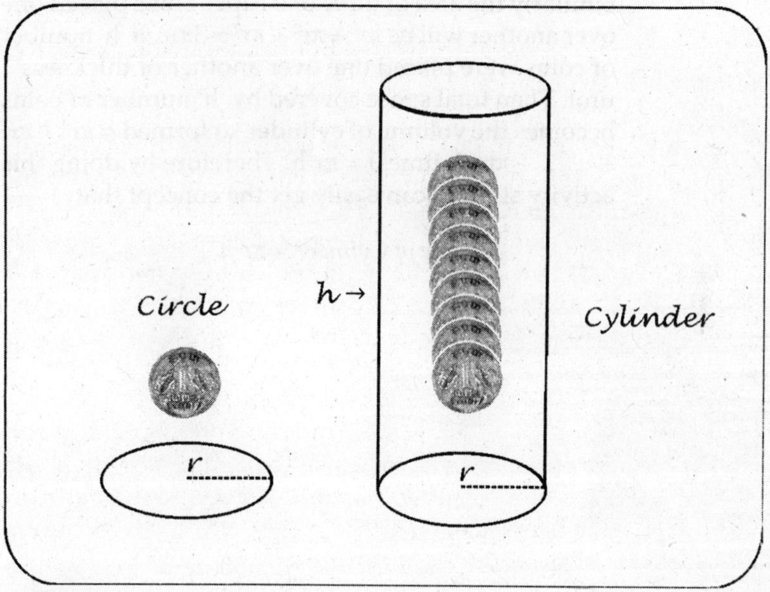

Activity

(i) *Material Required*: Coins.
(ii) *Description of the Activity*:

Concept of cylinder and its volume is not an easy task but can be made easier by the following activity:

- Concept of cylinder can be given by placing a number of similar circles exactly one over the other. For a circle a one rupee coin can be used. Thus, if we place a number of coins exactly one over the other, we get a cylinder, as shown in photograph.
- For giving the concept of volume of a cylinder, let the radius of this circle (coin) be 'r'. Students are asked to find out space covered by a one rupee coin by assuming that its thickness is 1 unit. Students have

the idea that it is equal to the area of circle *i.e.* πr^2. Now place another one rupee coin over the first one, so that the total space covered by these coins will be the sum of the area of two coins *i.e.* $\pi r^2 + \pi r^2 = 2\pi r^2$. Similarly the area of three one rupee coins placed one over another will be $\pi r^2 + \pi r^2 + \pi r^2 = 3\pi r^2$. If 'h' number of coins were placed one over another of thickness 1 unit. Then total space covered by 'h' number of coins becomes the volume of cylinder so formed = $\pi r^2 + \pi r^2 + \ldots\ldots + \pi r^2$ (h times) = $\pi r^2 h$. Therefore by doing this activity student can easily get the concept that:

Volume of Cylinder = $\pi r^2 h$

6.10 Balance

Rule: Weight: Weight is nothing but the comparison of things.

Activity

(i) *Material Required*: Real balance.

(ii) *Description of the Activity*:

Concept of balancing, equality and weight can be given by the use of balance. Students of the elementary classes have the nature of comparison very much *e.g.* they commonly use the sentences like: I am taller than you. He is heavier than me etc. By using this nature of students, teachers can give the concept of weight. By showing the see saw swing to the children and asking them as to how many children can balance me? Or how many stones can balance this packet of sand?

By giving such examples the teacher can easily give the concept about measurement of weight. The standard weight (real) can also be shown to the students. They can get the concept that *measurement of weight is nothing but the comparison of things with standard weight*.

7

Models

7.1 Introduction

Sometimes it is difficult for the teachers to take the real objects in the classroom, in such case they can take the help of models. Models are mainly representative copies or images of real objects. Any model can be defined as a simplified representation of a real situation. A mathematical model is a model created using mathematical tools. In order to clarify and explain the abstract concepts, something concrete like models have to be presented to explain those abstract concepts. These models help the students to grasp the point. Models also create interest in the students.

Models are two or three-dimensional representation of the real object. Teacher can provide plaster of paris and lime (*choona*) to students and ask them to make different types of solids *e.g.*, ball (sphere), cube, cuboids, cylinder, cone etc. By making these solids themselves, they can easily get the idea of these solid, their shapes, and their parts.

Some of the concepts that can be developed through the use of models are;

7.2 Base Value and Place Value

Rule: In a number, every digit has its particular place value.

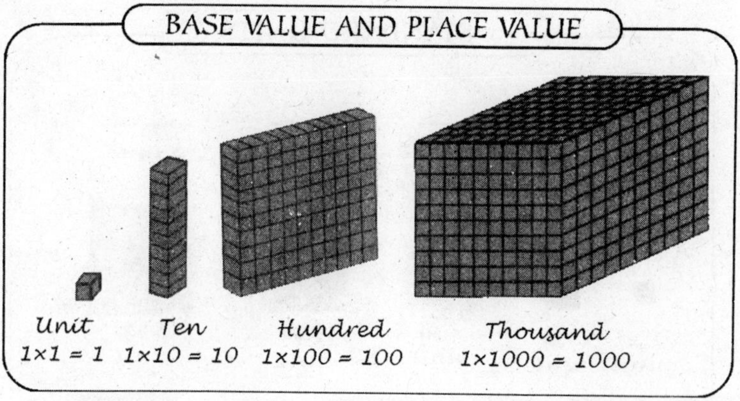

Activity

(i) *Material Required*: Cardboard, glazed paper, cubes made of chart paper.

(ii) *Description of the Activity*:

The concept of 'base value and place value' can be easily taught by a simple model. Students can be encouraged to make their own models to understand the concept of base value and place value. This model can be made as follows:

- Take a cardboard base and cover it with glazed paper. Take a cube and paste it on the base. It represents the 'unit' or' one'. Make a cubical rod of 10 cubes by fixing cubes on the above paper. Paste the rod on the base. These ten units combined to form a cuboidal rod of tens, represent 10 units or 1 ten. Take 10 cubical rods of the type (above mentioned) and place them on the base. Ten tens combined to form a solid of 100 units or ten tens or hundred. Make 10 solids of the type and paste them on the base. Ten hundreds combined together to form a cube of 10×10×10 *i.e.* 1 thousand. In this way students can get the concept that different digits in a number have different place values according to its position *e.g.* one's, ten's hundred's and they can find the value (place) of any number.

7.3 Standard Units

Rule: Relation between the units of length, area and volume.

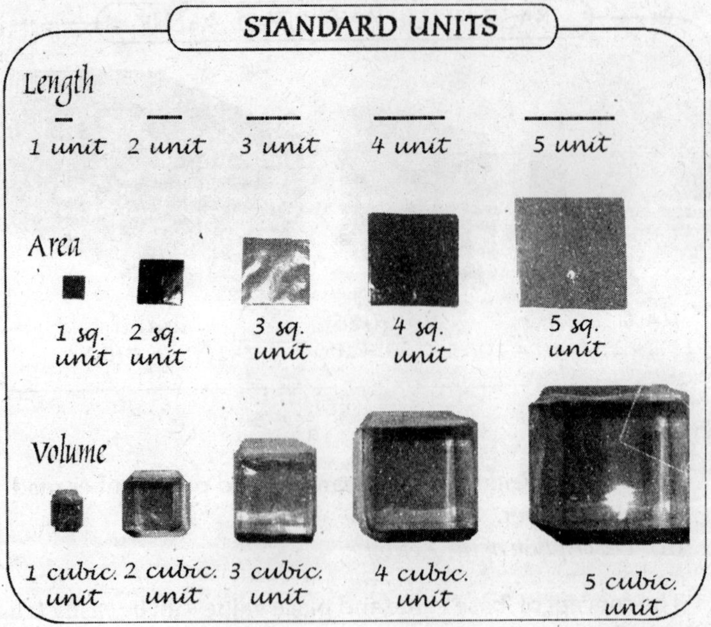

Activity

(i) *Material Required*: Cardboard, chart paper, cubes made of transparent sheet.

(ii) *Description of the Activity*:

Concept of standard unit and the relation between the units of length, area and volume can be easily taught with the help of the model shown in the above photograph. In this model sticks of different lengths *i.e.* 1 unit, 2 unit, 3 unit, 4 unit and 5 unit are displayed in the first row and the second row squares of sides 1 unit, 2 unit, 3 unit, 4 unit and 5 unit are displayed. This way their areas will be 1 sq. unit, 2 sq. unit, 3 sq. unit, 4 sq. unit and 5 sq. unit and in the third row cubes made by transparent sheets with sides 1 unit, 2 unit, 3 unit, 4 unit and 5 unit are displayed. Their volumes will be 1 cubic unit, 2 cubic unit, 3 cubic unit, 4 cubic unit and 5 cubic unit.

7.4 Number Line

Rule: Positive numbers always lie on the right hand side of zero and negative numbers are always on the left hand side of zero.

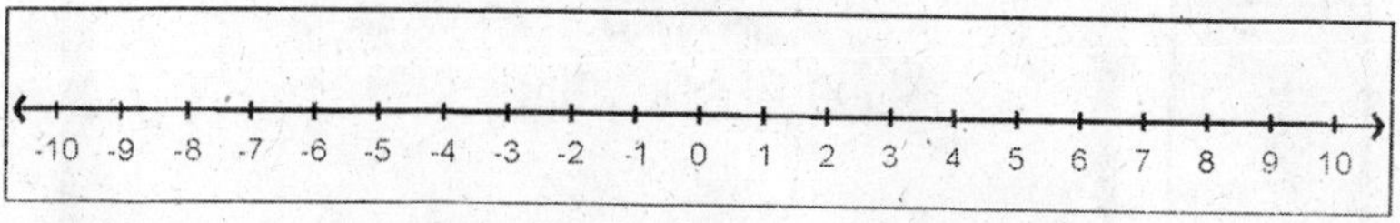

Activity

(i) *Material Required*: Chart paper.
(ii) *Description of the Activity*:

The child needs to know the basic facts of addition and multiplication very well, or will have difficulties with fractions, decimals, etc. These basic facts need to be known by heart. One of the best way to start children with math is to have them skip-count up and down from a very young age. Use a number line to show what 'skips' or 'steps' mean. Your child can master skip counting by two's, three's, four's, etc. with the help of the number line.

The concept of number line can easily be given by the model shown above.

7.5 Addition Ladder: A game for the beginners

Rule:

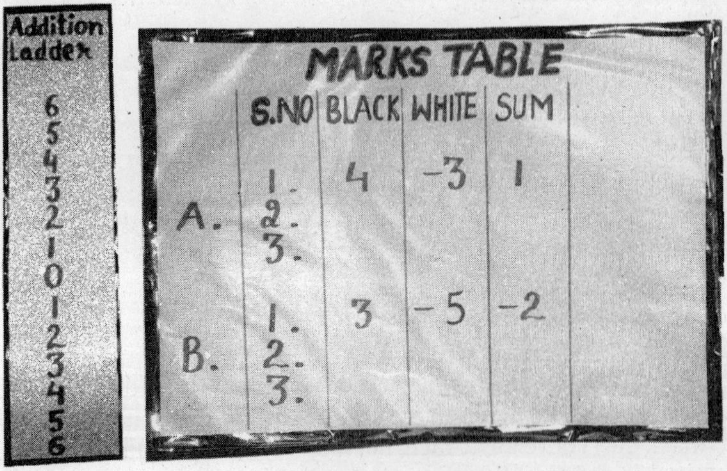

Activity

(i) *Material Required*: Ladder made of cardboard, one black and one white dice, coins. Chart for marks table.

(ii) *Description of the Activity:*

The model of addition ladder can be used as a game, to give the concept of addition of integers. In this game two dices one of black colour and the other of white colour is taken.

Let us suppose that black dice represent positive and white dice represent negative numbers. Both the dices are marked with numbers 1 to 6. Before starting the game children place their respective coins at 0 in the addition ladder. The rules of the game are as follows:

1. For each positive number, move upwards and for each negative number move downwards.
2. Each player has to begin from 0.
3. Each player has to find out his final score from the marks table. Whoever secures more marks wins the game.

The game can be played like this:

One child throws both the dices, if the number is 4 on the black dice, it represents +4, and 3 on white, it represents –3. So to know his sum first he moves upward +4 from 0 on the ladder, then moves 3 steps downward and reaches '1'. Then he writes this score in his marks table 'A'.

Now second child throws the dice. Let the number is 3 on the black dice and 5 on the white one. Like the first child he too moves upwards by 3 steps and then moves downward by 5 steps, and reaches –2. He writes this score in marks table 'B'. The process goes on and the marks obtained are filled in their respective tables. You can write their respective scores at the marks table drawn on the cardboard. In the end add all the sums, the child who got the highest marks win the game.

7.6 Properties of Numbers

Rule: Let a, b, c are different numbers.

1. If a = b then a + c = b + c
2. a + b = b + a (Commutative Law)
3. (a + b) + c = a + (b + c) (Associative Law)
4. If a = b then, 5a = 5b

Activity

(i) *Material Required*: Model of balance.
(ii) *Description of the Activity*:

Different properties of numbers like Commutative and associative properties and also many others properties of numbers can be taught with the help of the model of a balance and weights where weights can represents different numbers. For example—

1. If a = b then a + c = b + c
2. a + b = b + a
3. (a + b) + c = a + (b + c)
4. If a = b, then 5a = 5b
5. If a = b, then ac = bc etc.

Where a, b, c are different weight.

Concept of equation can also be easily given by the use of balance.

7.7 Proof of $(a + b)^3$

Rule: $(a + b)^3 = a^3 + b^3 + 3a^2b + 3ab^2$

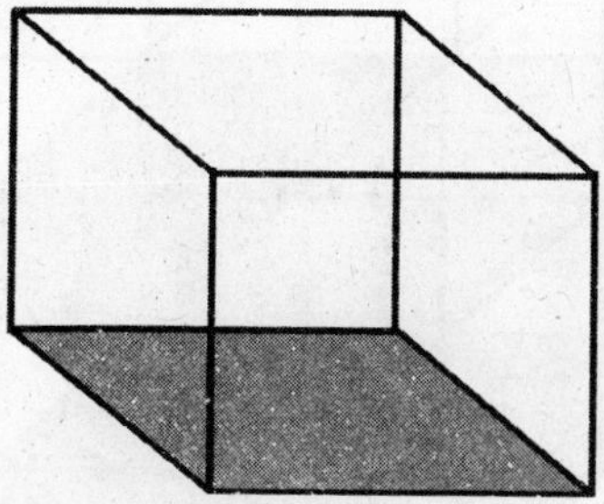

a^3

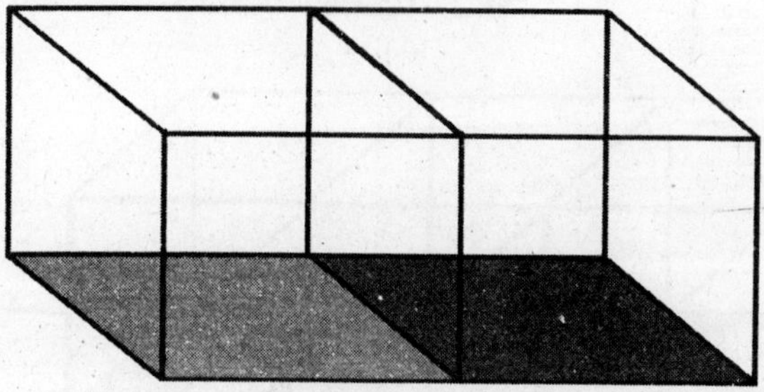

a^2b

ab^2

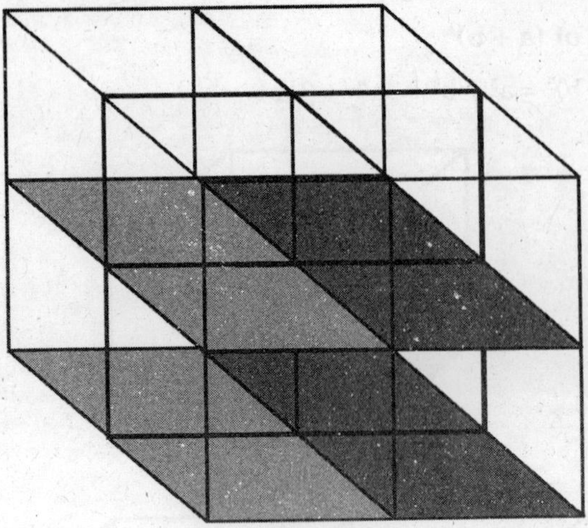

b^3

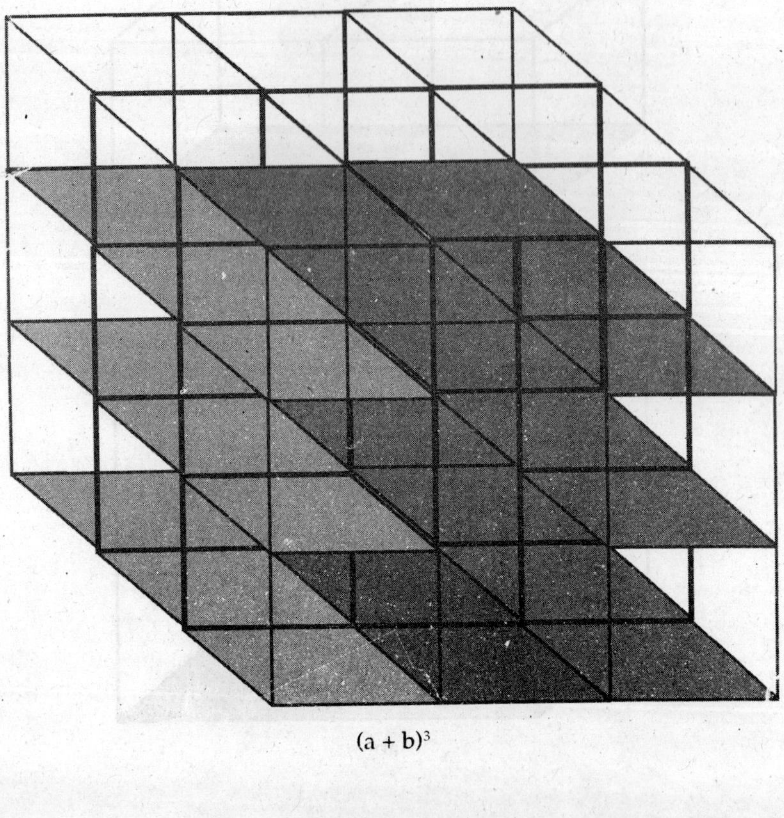

$(a + b)^3$

Activity

(i) *Material Required*: Blocks.

(ii) *Description of the Activity*:

The following activity is performed to verify the formula; $(a + b)^3 = a^3 + b^3 + 3a^2b + 3ab^2$.

For the purpose of verification we will take few blocks (playing blocks) and let us start with an example of supposing our 'a' as '1', and 'b' as '2' *i.e.*, $a = 1, b = 2$.

Then what will be the cube of 'a' *i.e.*, cube of 1.

Obviously it will be 1, so we will only need one block for the purpose of representing cube of 'a' *i.e.* cube of 1 since blocks available to us are in cubic shape only.

Therefore $a^3 = 1^3 = 1$ block.

Now let us find the cube of b, since the term involved in expanded formula involves b^3 as well. Obviously cube of 2 (that is cube of b) is 8, which means we will need 8 blocks. Thus, $b^3 = 2^3 = 8$ = 8 blocks arranged in the form of cube of 2 such that there are 2 blocks each length-wise, breadth-wise and width-wise respectively.

Next in the expression we have terms like $3a^2b$ which will be equal to, $a^2b = 1 \times 1 \times 2 = 2$

i.e. there shall be cuboid comprising of 2 blocks. Therefore $a^2b = 2 = 2$ blocks. Thus, we will need 3 pairs of 2 blocks each so that we get $3a^2b$.

Next we could see that formula involves terms like $3ab^2$ *i.e.* we will need to calculate ab^2.

Therefore $ab^2 = 1 \times 2 \times 2 = 4 = 4$ blocks *i.e.* we shall be requiring 3 sets of 4 blocks each to represent our $3ab^2$. Therefore $ab^2 = 4 = 4$ blocks.

Now let us combine all these blocks together. These blocks have pins at their ends so that these can be fixed one inside the other or can be joined/attached to each other easily.

Let us see the arrangement we obtain after joining them and then count the total number of blocks, which has made that arrangement.

Thus, we see that all blocks together constitute a cube of 27 blocks *i.e.*,

27 = cube of 3 (because it constituted a cube of length, breadth and width of side 3cm each).

$$= (3)^3$$
$$= (1 + 2)^3$$

Therefore $(a + b)^3 = a^3 + b^3 + 3a^2b + 3ab^2$

Hence, the result is verified.

7.8 Concept of Integers

Rule: Integers is the set of numbers that contains whole numbers as well as negative numbers.

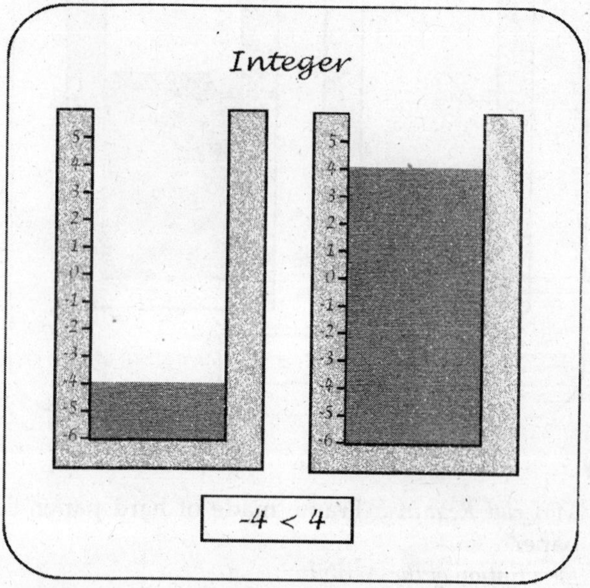

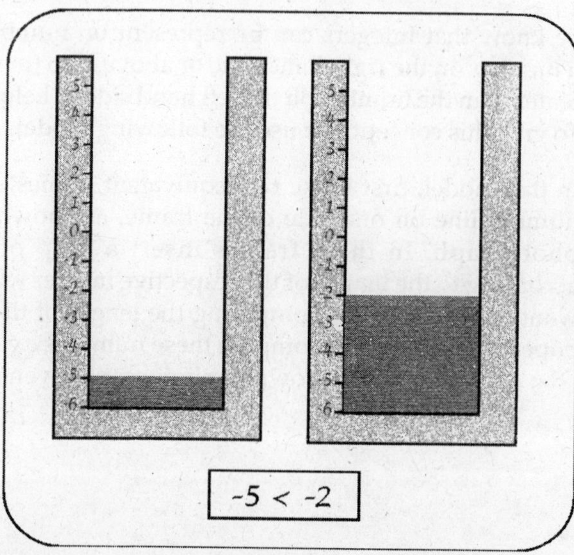

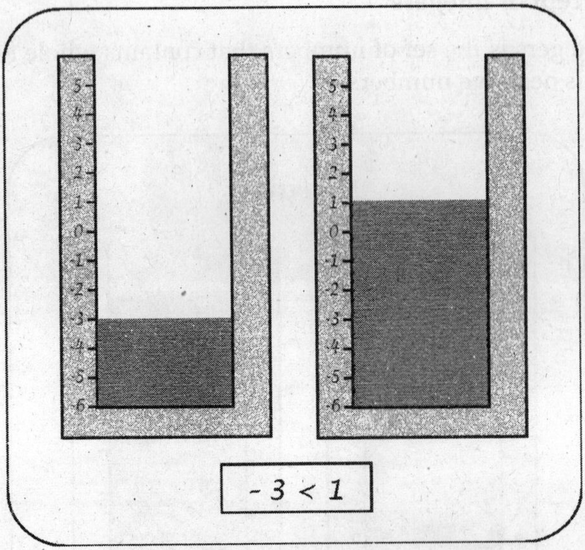

Activity

(i) *Material Required*: Frame made of hard paper, coloured paper.

(ii) *Description of the Activity*:

As we know that integers can be represent on number line. And each number on the right hand side or above zero (in vertical line) is greater than the number on the left hand side or below zero.

To give this concept, we use the following model:

➢ In this model, first make two equivalent frames, make a number line on one side of the frame, as shown in the photograph. In these frames insert a strip of paper according to the length of the respective integer which we want to represent. By comparing the length of these two papers, one can easily compare these numbers *e.g.*, $-4 < 4$, $-5 < -2$, $-3 < 1$ etc. as shown in photograph given above.

7.9 Concept of Addition of Integers

Rule: Numbers with same sign (positive or negative) are added and numbers with different sign are subtracted.

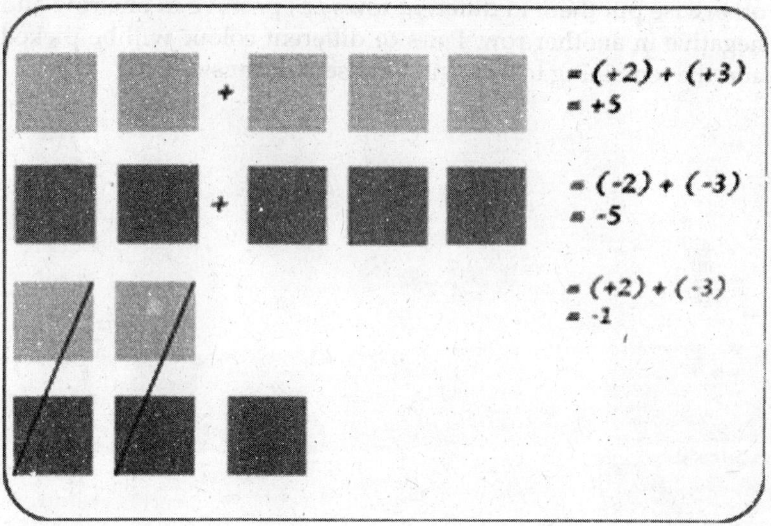

Activity

(i) *Material Required*: 25 small square pieces of papers. These pieces are of red colour from one side and of white colour on the other side.

(ii) *Description of the Activity*:

Concept of operations of integers can be explained with the help of the following activity:

➢ The whole class is divided in small groups and each group is provided with a packet of integers, in which there are (say) 25 small square pieces of paper. These pieces are of red colour from one side and of white colour on the other side. Let us suppose that red colour represents ' +1' and white colour represents '–1'.

Rules of the Activity

For positive numbers put the tokens from red side and for negative numbers put the tokens from white side. If the numbers are of the same type (sign) then put the tokens in one row and count them otherwise put them in different rows *i.e.,* positive in one row and negative in another row. Pairs of different colour will be picked and the remaining tokens will represent the answer.

7.10 Fractions

Rule: Fractions can be defined as a part of a whole or as a part of a group.

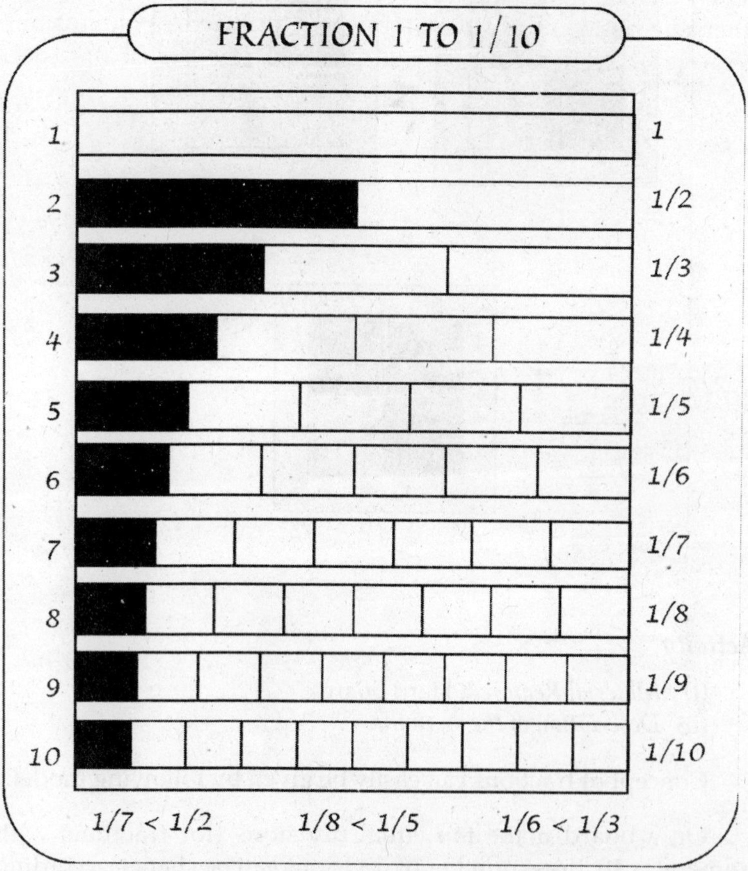

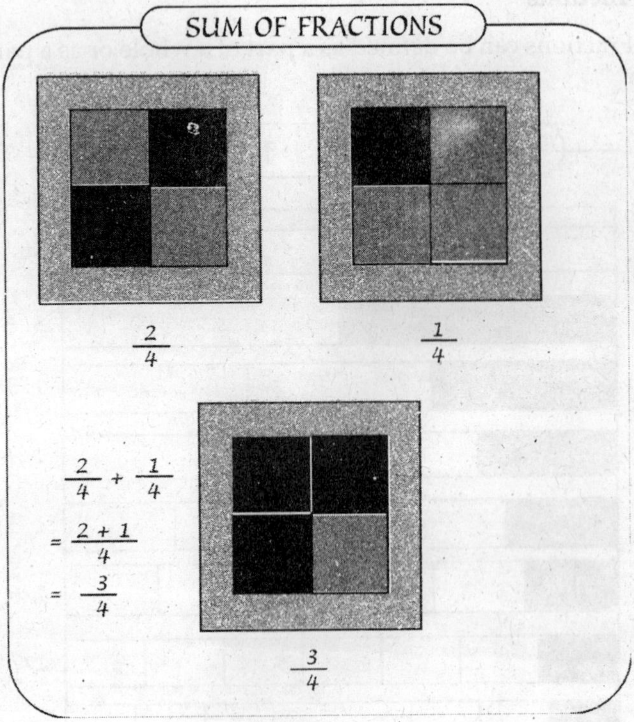

Activity

(i) *Material Required*: Hard board

(ii) *Description of the Activity*:

Concept of fractions can easily be given by following model:

On a board make ten equal divisions (for fractions with numerator 10, these number of divisions can be change according to the numerator of different fractions), after that in these divisions insert the strips according to the fractions, as shown in photograph. Through this model concept of fraction can be easily taught, as well as comparison of fractions can also be easily taught.

For addition of fractions another model can be used. In this model, take different squares of same size, and divide it into equivalent parts *e.g.* if we want to give the concept that $^2/_4 + ¼ = ¾$, then each square will be divide into four equivalent parts, and then ¼ and $^2/_4$ can be easily shown. By adding this we get ¾ as shown in photograph.

7.11 Solids

Rule: Concept of cube, cuboids, sphere, cone, cylinder, prism.

Activity

(i) *Material Required*: Cardboard or chart paper.

(ii) *Description of the Activity*:

Models of geometrical solid such as cube, cuboids, sphere, cone, cylinder, prism etc., may be made out of cardboard or chart paper and may be used to give the concept of these shapes and its parts. They may also be used to teach topics such as surface area and volumes of those solids.

7.12 Geoboard

Rule: Different geometrical shapes and their properties, concept of area.

Activity

(i) *Material Required*: Board of wood, ply wood, plastic or hard card boards, nails, rubber bands.
(ii) *Description of the Activity*:

Different geometrical shapes and concept of area can easily be given with the help of a geoboard. Geoboard is an instrument made on a board of wood, ply wood, plastic or hard card board, by piercing nails on it at equal distance. The nails are pierced in such a way that their ¾ parts are visible and ¼ parts remain inserted in the board. By placing thin round elastic (rubber band) in the nails, we can make and show different shapes like angle, triangle, quadrilateral, pentagon, hexagon, parallelogram, rhombus, square and rectangle etc. in the classroom. Different properties and different types of these figures can also be shown easily on the geoboard *e.g.*, different types of angles like right angle, acute angle, obtuse angle etc., and different types of lines like parallel lines, intersecting lines etc. can also be shown easily on the geoboard. Different properties of geometrical figures like 'opposite sides of a rectangle are equal', (by counting the nails) and that 'the diagonals of the rhombus bisect each other at right angle' can be studies easily. Difficult concepts like circumference and area can also be taught with the help of a geoboard. If we want to make a triangle of area $6cm^2$, then the elastic should cover 3 nails on one side, 4 nails on the second side and 5 nails on the third side. In this way geoboard is a very effective teaching aid.

7.13 Types of angles

Rule: An angle is made up of two rays starting from a common end point.

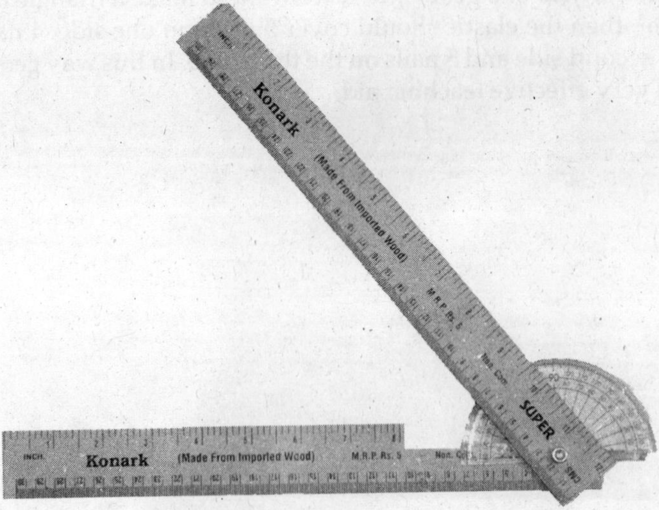

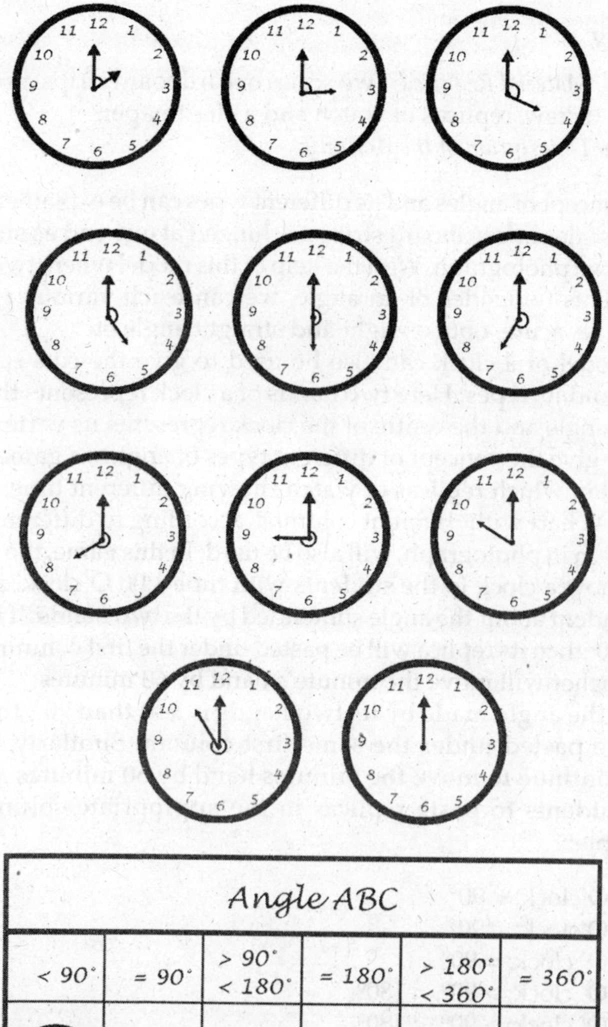

Angle ABC					
< 90°	= 90°	> 90° < 180°	= 180°	> 180° < 360°	= 360°

Activity

(i) *Material Required*: Two scales or cardboard strips, protector, screw, replicas of watch and a chart paper.

(ii) *Description of the Activity*:

Concept of angles and its different types can be explained easily if two scales or cardboard strips are hinged at one end as shown in the above photograph. With the help of this model where two scales represents two sides of an angle, we can teach various types of angles *i.e.* acute, obtuse, right and straight angle etc.

Model of a clock can also be used to give the concept of an angle and its types. Here two hands of a clock represents the sides of the angle and the centre of the clock represents its vertex.

To give the concept of different types of angles, a game can be played in which replicas of watch showing different times can be used. A chart with different columns, according to different types, as shown in photograph, will also be used. In this game, the teacher will show a clock to the students with time 1:00 O'clock, and ask the student about the angle subtended by the two hands. If it is less than 90º then its replica will be pasted under the first column. Then, the teacher will move the minute's hand by 60 minutes.

If the angle made by its two hands is less than 90º, then this will be pasted under the same first column. Similarly teacher will continue to move the minutes hand by 60 minutes and ask the students to paste replicas in the appropriate column. For example:

1 O'clock: < 90°
2 O'clock: < 90°
3 O' clock: = 90º
4 O' clock: > 90º, < 180º
5 O' clock: > 90º, < 180º
6 O' clock: = 180º
7 O' clock: > 180º, < 360º
8 O' clock: > 180º, < 360º
9 O' clock: >180º, < 360°
10 O' clock: > 180º, < 360°
11 O' clock: > 180º, < 360°
12 O' clock: =360º

Then, with the help of this activity teacher will explain different types of angles as follows:

1. An angle whose measure is equal to 90º is called a *right angle.*
2. An angle whose measure is equal to 180º is called a *straight angle.*
3. An angle whose measure is equal to 360º is called a *complete angle.*
4. An angle whose measure is greater than 0º and lesser than 90º is called an *acute angle.*
5. An angle whose measure is greater than 90º and lesser than 180º is called an *obtuse angle.*
6. An angle whose measure is greater than 180º and lesser than 360º is called a *reflex angle.*

7.14 Vertically Opposite Angles

Rule: If two lines intersect then the vertically opposite angles are equal.

Activity

(i) *Material Required*: Ice cream sticks.

(ii) *Description of the Activity*:

Following activity was performed for teaching vertically opposite angles:

- All the students in the class were provided with two ice cream sticks each, labelled AB and CD intersecting at the point O. These were arranged in such a way that they formed the shape similar to that of alphabet X, as shown in photograph.
- Then students were asked to rotate the stick AB about the point O until OB fell along OD. Then the students were asked to observe:
  Does OA also fall along OC?
  The students were easily observed this that OA falls along OC.
- Then teacher asked the students.
  What can we infer about $\angle AOC$ & $\angle BOD$?

- After listening to different responses the teacher told the students that the amount of rotation from OB to OD is the same as amount of rotation from OA to OC. This means both have swept equal angles.

In other, words $\angle AOC \cong \angle BOD$

Thus we can infer that *if two lines intersect then the vertically opposite angles are equal.*

This activity can also be done with the help of two pencils tied at the center with the help of rubber bands.

7.15 Pairs of Angles

Rule:

- *Adjacent Angles*: Two angles with a common arm are known as adjacent angles.
- *Linear Pair*: Two adjacent angles whose sum is 180° are known as linear pair.

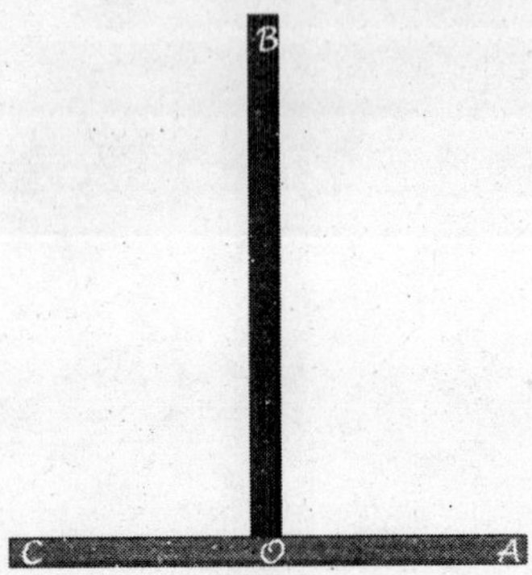

Activity

(i) *Material Required*: Card board, glazed paper, pins.
(ii) *Description of the Activity*:

Different pairs of angles such as adjacent angles, linear pairs, complementary and supplementary angles can be easily explained with the help of the models made by card board strips. Three card board strips were given to each student and they were asked to make these pairs of angles.

7.16 Parallel Lines Intersected by a Transversal

Rule: If two parallel lines are intersected by a transversal, then

1. each pair of corresponding angles are equal.
2. each pair of alternate angles are equal.

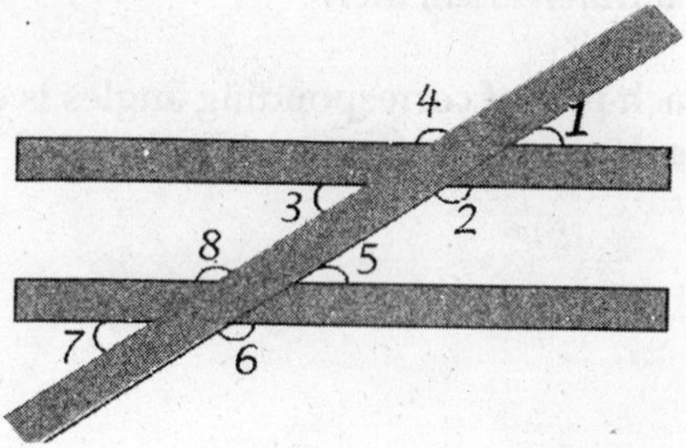

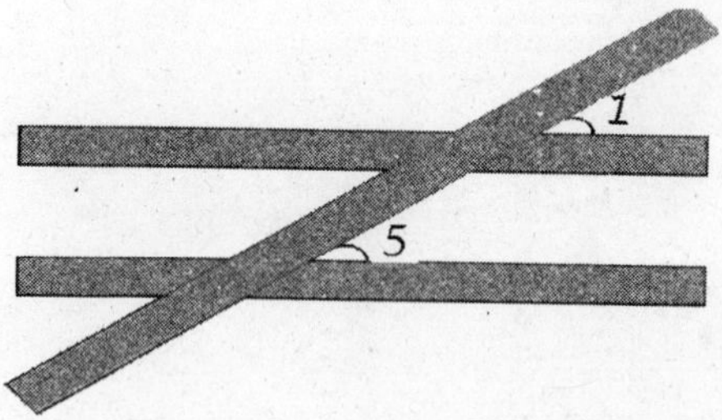

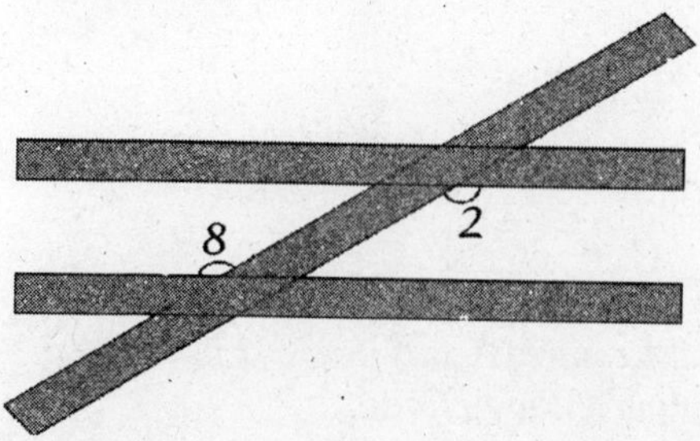

Activity

(i) *Material Required*: Card board, glazed paper, pins.
(ii) *Description of the Activity*:

This concept can easily be understood with the help of the

above model. To make this model, take three card board strips and arrange two of them in such a way that they are parallel to each other and keep the third in such a way that it intersects the other two. Now ask the students to measure all the eight angles and find the relationship between them. With the help of this activity students can easily get the concept that, 'if two parallel lines are intersected by a transversal, then

1. each pair of corresponding angles is equal.
2. each pair of alternate angles is equal.

7.17 Angle Sum Property of a Triangle

Rule: Sum of three angles of a triangle is 180°.

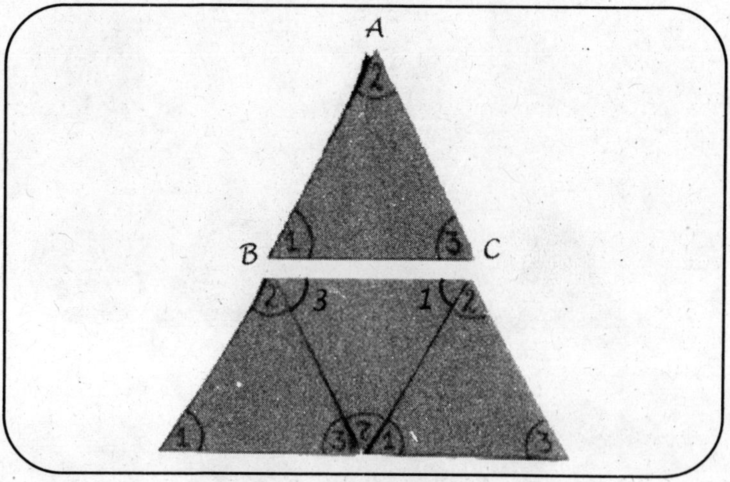

Fig. 1

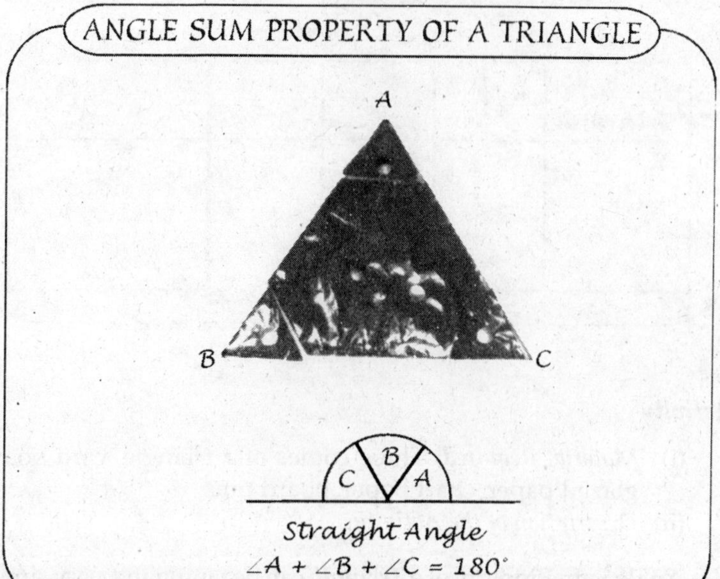

Fig. 2

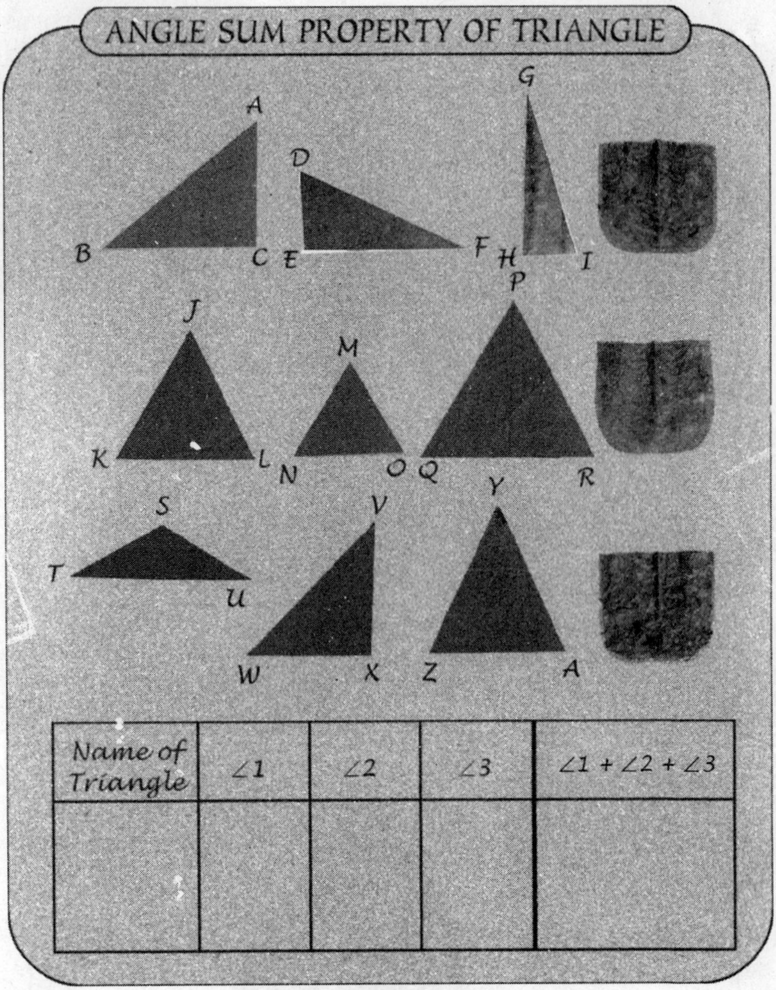

Fig. 3

Activity

(i) *Material Required*: Three copies of a triangle, card board, glazed paper, chart paper, board pins.

(ii) *Description of the Activity*:

Angle Sum Property of a Triangle can be taught in a very simple way with the help of following activities:

Make three copies of any triangle say ΔABC. Arrange them as shown in the photograph (Fig. 1). Now ask the students, what do they observe about ∠1 + ∠2 + ∠3. They can easily observe that *∠1 + ∠2 + ∠3 = 180° or the sum of three angles of the triangle is 180º*, because they make a straight line.

A simple model can also be made to explain this property. For this take a triangle made by card board, cut its three angles and attach them with the triangle with the help of board pins on a hard board as shown in the photograph (Fig. 2). Below the triangle draw a line with any point O at it. Now ask the students to take out the angles and arrange them at O in such a way that there should not be any overlapping, and the vertex of each angle should falls on O and observe its result.

A game can also be played to attain this concept. For this different types of triangles can be made on a black board or on a chart. Ask the students to measure the angles and fill up the table as shown in the photograph (Fig. 3) and find out their sum, and observe the result.

7.18 Sum of Two Sides of a Triangle is Greater than the Third Side

Rule: Sum of two sides of a triangle is greater than the third side

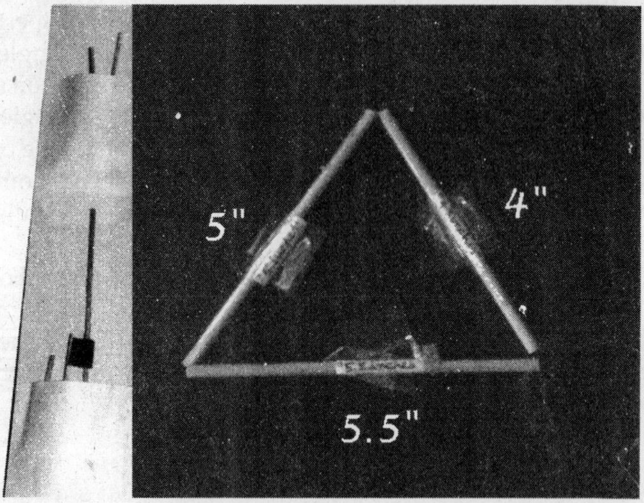

Activity

(i) *Material Required*: Hard board, black sticky tape, sticks.
(ii) *Description of the Activity*:

This concept can easily be taught with the help of the model shown in the photograph. To make this model take ten equal strips of 10 inches each of black tape and paste them side by side to make a square on a hard board, as shown in the photograph. Then take a number of sticks of different lengths, measure each stick and write its measurement (length) on it. Paste a small piece of sticky tape on the stick to enable it to stick on the square made on the board. Make a pocket of paper on one side of the square on the board and put these sticks in this pocket.

Ask the students to take any three sticks from the pocket and try to make triangles by sticking them on the square in such a way that end points of the sticks should meet. Repeat the activity by choosing different sizes of sticks. From this activity students can easily get the concept that,' *the sum of any two sides of a triangle is greater than the third side*'.

7.19 Exterior Angle of a Triangle is Equal to the Sum of Its Interior Opposite Angles

Rule: Exterior Angle of a Triangle is equals to the sum of its interior opposite angles.

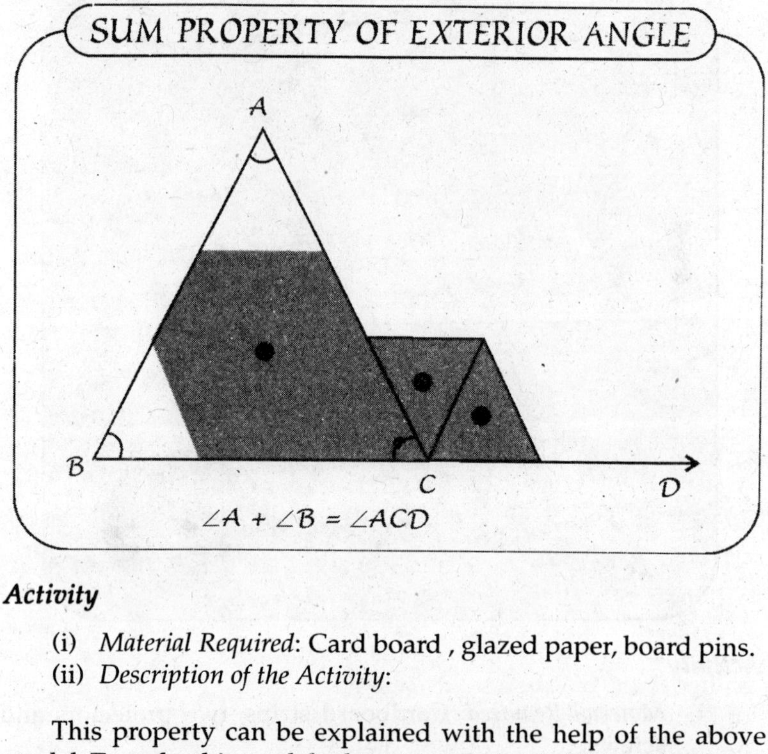

Activity

(i) *Material Required*: Card board , glazed paper, board pins.
(ii) *Description of the Activity*:

This property can be explained with the help of the above model. To make this model take a triangle (say) ABC made of card board, cut its two interior angles (say) A&B and attach them along the triangle with the help of board pins on a hard board and extend its one side (say) BC as shown in the photograph. Now ask the students to take out these two angles and arrange them at C in such a way that there should not be any overlapping, and the vertex of each angle falls at O and observe its result. Students can easily observe that the *sum of two interior opposite angles of a triangle is equal to its exterior angle*.

7.20 Types of Triangle

Rule: A closed figure made up by three line segments is known as a triangle.

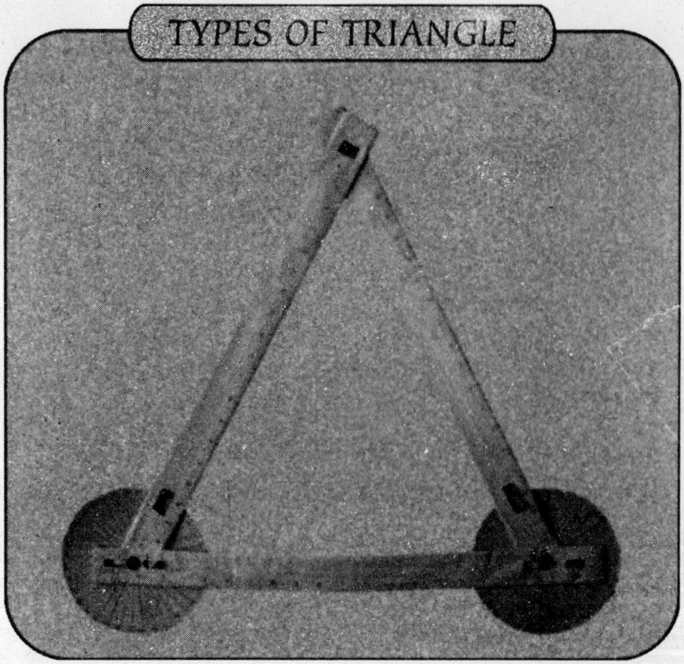

Activity

(i) *Material Required*: Cardboard strips, two protectors and screws.
(ii) *Description of the Activity*:

Types of triangle can easily be taught with the help of the above model.

Make three rulers scales on the strips of a cardboard. Attach two protectors and two strips on each corner of the third strip with the help of screws, as shown in the photograph. The upper ends of the strips are not fixed. By moving these two strips, different types of triangles, based on sides as well as based on angles, can be easily taught.

7.21 Verification of Pythagoras Theorem

Rule: (Hypotenuse)^2 = (Perpendicular)^2 + (Base)^2

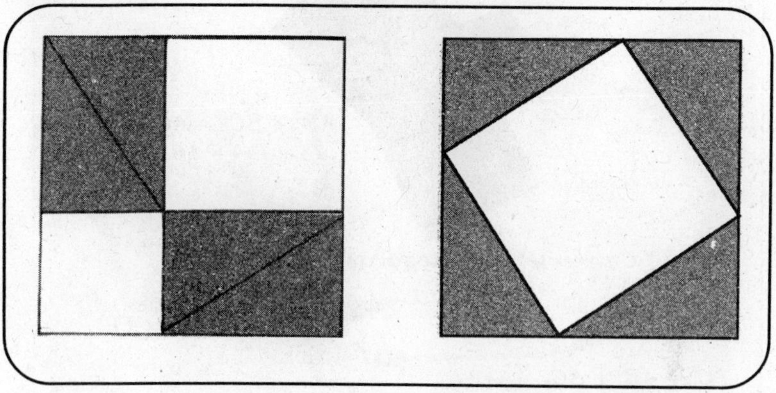

Fig. 1

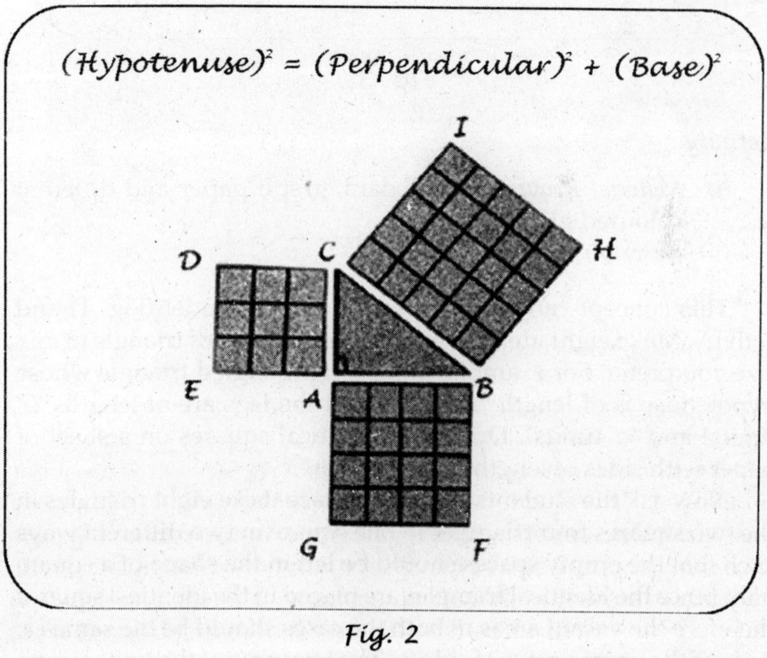

Fig. 2

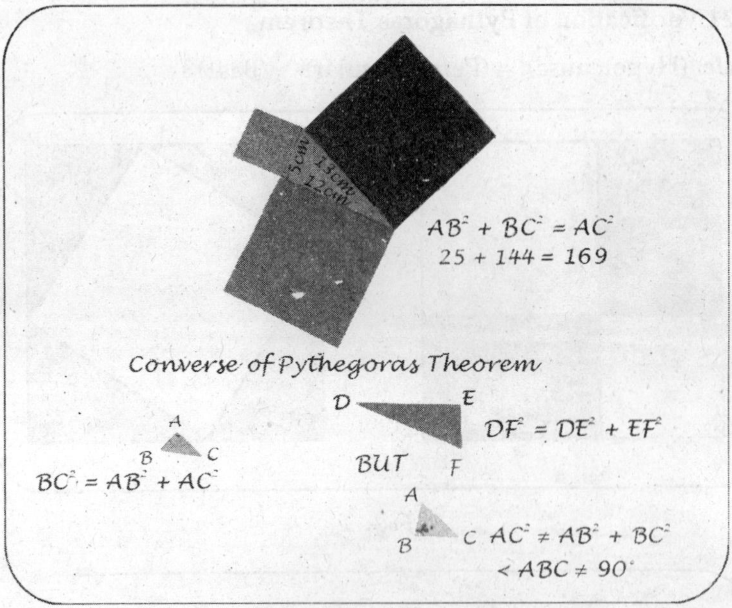

Fig. 3

Activity

(i) *Material Required*: Cardboard, graph paper and different coloured glazed papers.

(ii) *Description of the Activity*:

This concept can be given by the above model (Fig. 1) and activity. Make eight identical copies of right-angles triangle of any size you prefer. For example, make a right-angled triangle whose hypotenuse is of length 'a' (units) and the legs are of lengths 'b' (units) and 'c' (units). Draw two identical squares on a sheet of paper with sides of length 'b + c' (units).

Now ask the students to try and place these eight triangles in the two squares four triangles in one square in two different ways such that the empty spaces should be left in the shape of a square only. Since the identical triangles are placed in the identical squares therefore the vacant areas in both the cases should be the same *i.e.* Area of the inner square of side a =The total area of the two squares of sides b and c each *i.e.*,

$$a^2 = b^2 + c^2$$

Another model (Fig. 2) can be made to give this concept. Draw a triangle with sides 3, 4 and 5 units, on a card board. Now make squares on each side of the triangle, then ask the students to count the squares on each side and think about the above property.

Converse of this theorem can also be taught with the help of a model as shown in the photograph (Fig. 3).

7.22 Types of Quadrilaterals

Rule: Different types of quadrilaterals such as parallelogram, square, rectangle, trapezium, parallelogram etc.

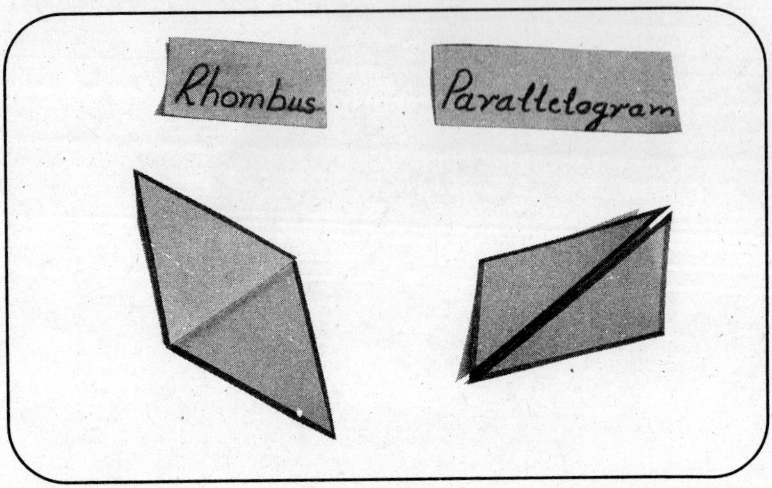

Activity

(i) *Material Required*: Four identical triangles of each type *i.e.* equilateral, isosceles, scalene, right, acute and obtuse triangle in such a way that in each triangle the equal parts are shown with same colour.

(ii) *Description of the Activity*:

The above model and activity can easily give the concept of different types of quadrilaterals.

Make four identical triangles of each type *i.e.*, equilateral, isosceles, scalene, right, acute and obtuse triangle in such a way that in each triangle the equal parts are shown with same colour as shown in the photograph. Now ask the students to make different types of quadrilaterals with the help of these triangles *e.g.* by joining two isosceles triangles a rhombus can be made or by joining two scalene triangles a parallelogram can be made. Now observe this quadrilaterals and find out its properties. Try to make different types of quadrilaterals and study its properties.

7.23 Angle Sum Property of a Quadrilateral

Rule: Sum of four angles of a quadrilateral is 360°.

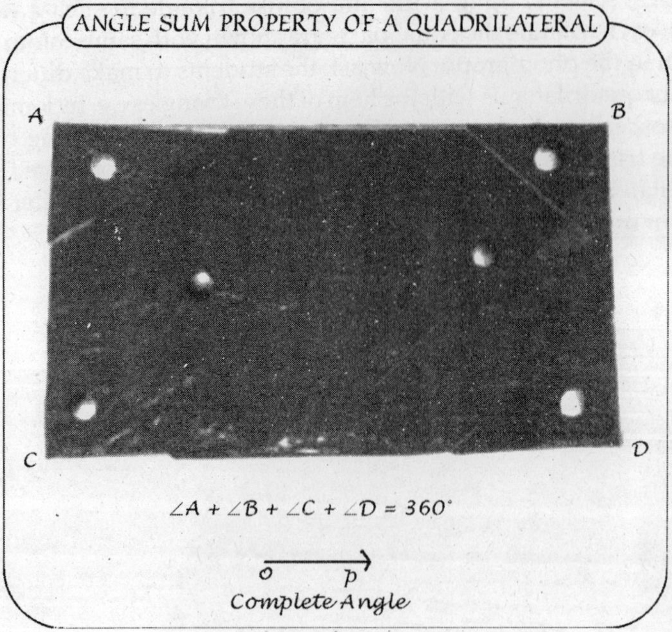

Activity

(i) *Material Required*: A quadrilateral made by cardboard or thick paper, mount board, board pins.

(ii) *Description of the Activity*:

Angle sum property of quadrilateral can be taught in a very simple way with the help of the following activity:

A quadrilateral made by cardboard or thick paper was used here. The four angles of the quadrilateral were cut and attached them with the quadrilateral with the help of board pines on a mount board as shown in photograph. Below the quadrilateral, draw a ray OP with initial point O. Ask the students to take out the angles and arranged them at O in such a way that there should not be any overlapping, and the vertex of each angle falls on O. Now ask the students, what do you observe about ∠1 + ∠2 + ∠3 + ∠4. They can easily observe that *the sum of four angles of the quadrilateral is 360°*.

7.24 Exterior Angle Property of a Polygon

Rule: Sum of exterior angles of a polygon is 360°.

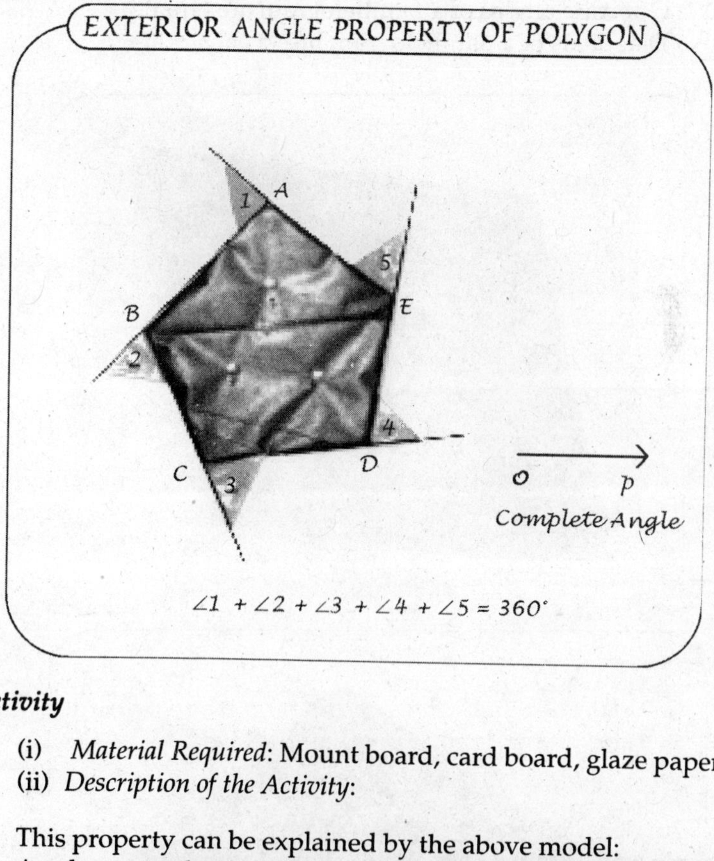

Activity

(i) *Material Required*: Mount board, card board, glaze paper.
(ii) *Description of the Activity*:

This property can be explained by the above model:

A polygon made of card board labelled as ABCDE with exterior angles marked as $\angle 1$, $\angle 2$, $\angle 3$, $\angle 4$ and $\angle 5$ was pasted on the mount board. The five exterior angles of the polygon were cut and attached to it with the help of board pins on the mount board as shown in the photograph. Below the polygon draw a ray OP with initial point O. Ask the students to take out the angles and arranged them at O in such a way that there isn't any overlapping, and the vertex of each angle falls on O. Now ask the students, what they observe about $\angle 1 + \angle 2 + \angle 3 + \angle 4 + \angle 5$. They can easily understand that *the sum of exterior angles of a polygon is 360°*.

7.25 Properties of a Parallelogram

Rule: The properties of a parallelogram are as follows:

1. Opposite sides of a parallelogram are equal.
2. Opposite angles of a parallelogram are equal.
3. Diagonals of a parallelogram bisect each other.

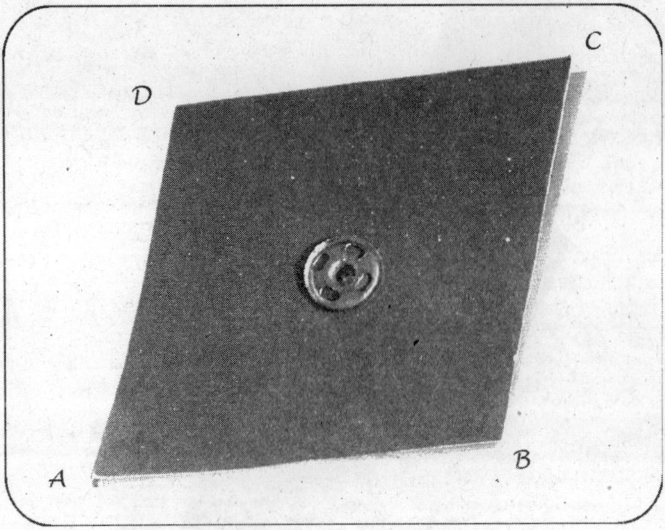

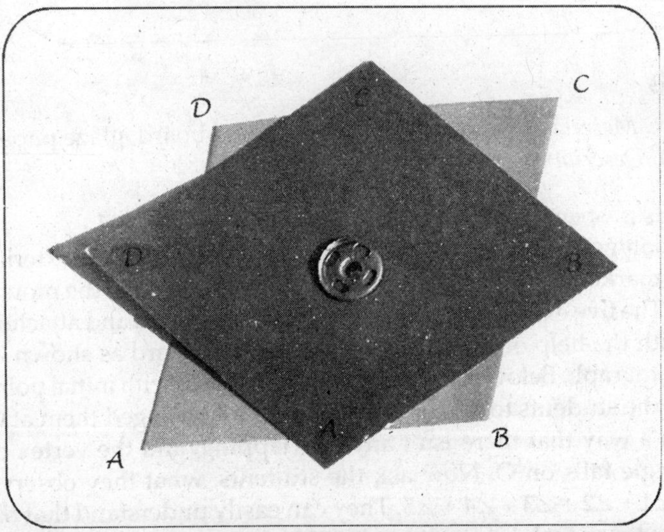

Activity

(i) *Material Required*: Two congruent parallelograms made of cardboard or thick sheet.

(ii) *Description of the Activity*:

Properties of a parallelogram can easily be taught by the following activity:

- Draw a parallelogram say ABCD on a cardboard or thick sheet of paper and join its diagonal AC and BD to intersect at point O. Draw another parallelogram congruent to the first parallelogram. Label it as ABCD again. Let its diagonals AC and BD also intersect at the point O.
- Now place the second parallelogram over the first by fixing a pin or nail at the point O so that both the parallelograms cover each other completely under the correspondence ABCD⇔ABCD.
- Now let us rotate the upper parallelogram about the point O so that its vertex A comes to the position of vertex C of the other parallelogram. You will observe that vertex B comes to the position of vertex D of the other parallelogram.
- Similarly, vertex C comes to the position of vertex A and D comes to the position of vertex B of the other parallelogram. You can further note that in this position the two parallelograms cover each other completely.

Thus, we may say that:

1. AB = CD and AD = BC
2. $\angle A = \angle C$ and $\angle B = \angle D$
3. OA = OC and OB = OD

In words, we can say that:

1. *Opposite sides of a parallelogram are equal.*
2. *Opposite angles of a parallelogram are equal.*
3. *Diagonals of a parallelogram bisect each other.*

7.26 Congruence of Figures

Rule: Figures having same shape and size are called congruent figures and congruent figures completely cover each other.

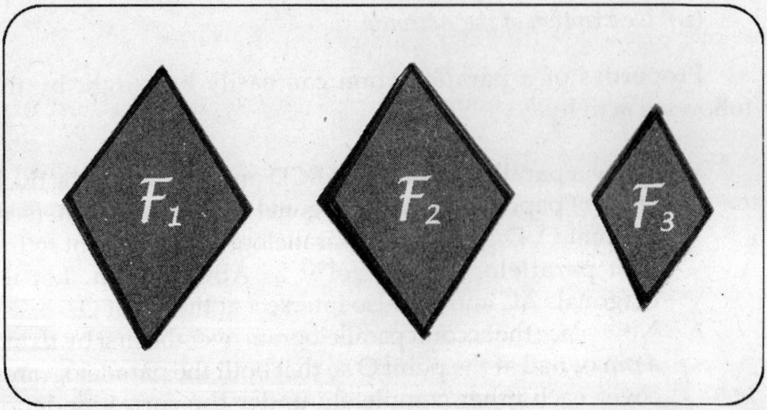

Activity

(i) *Material Required*: Two congruent figures F_1 & F_2 and another figure F_3 which is of the same shape but of different size made of cardboard or thermocol or thick sheet of paper.

(ii) *Description of the Activity*:

Following activity can be performed to give the concept of congruence. Suppose we have three figures F_1, F_2 and F_3 (diamond shaped). To check weather these are congruent or not, we place one figure over the other (say F_1 over F_2). While placing F_1 over F_2, we have permitted the following motions:

1. Sliding in the plane without rotation.
2. Rotation about a point in the plane.
3. Inverting upside down.

We are not permitted any other motion like bending, stretching and twisting.

With these three types of motions mentioned above, we try to move F_1 so as to cover F_2. If F_1covers F_2 exactly then F_1 and F_2 must be of same shape and size. Therefore, we can say that F_1 is congruent to F_2.

Again using three types of motions mentioned above, if we try to move F_1 to cover F_3, we will find that F_1 will not cover F_3 exactly. This means that F_1 and F_3 are not congruent. (Although they have the same shape)

Therefore, F_3 is not congruent to F_1.

This method of comparing figures is called method of *superposition.*

Thus, a plane figure F_1 is said to be congruent to F_2, if F_1, when superimposed over F_2, covers it exactly. Symbol $\cong$ is used to indicate "is congruent to".

Thus when F_1 is congruent to F_2, we write it as—

$F_1 \cong F_2$ and read it as fig. F_1 is congruent to fig. F_2

And when F_1 is not congruent to F_3, we write it as $F_1 \ncong F_3$.

7.27 Angle in a Semicircle is a Right Angle

Rule: Angle in a Semicircle is a Right Angle

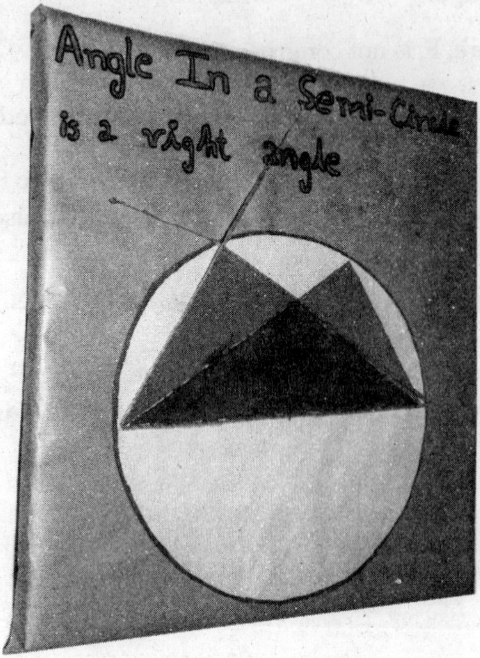

Activity

(i) *Material Required*: Mount board, glass rods or pipes, thread.

(ii) *Description of the Activity*:

This concept can be easily taught with the help of the above model.

In this model a circle is drawn on a mount board. Three glass pipes are strung in a thread. The middle glass pipe is glued on the diameter, and the other two pipes act as line segments. Then, by moving the thread, the students are asked to try and make the two pipes meet at a common point on any point on the circumference of the semicircle and observe the angle made by these pipes in the semicircle (two such angles are shown in the photograph). By repeating this activity many times students can easily get the concept that angle in a semicircle is a right angle.

7.28 Equal Intercept Property

Rule: If three parallel lines make equal intercepts on one transversal, then they make equal intercepts on any other transversal as well.

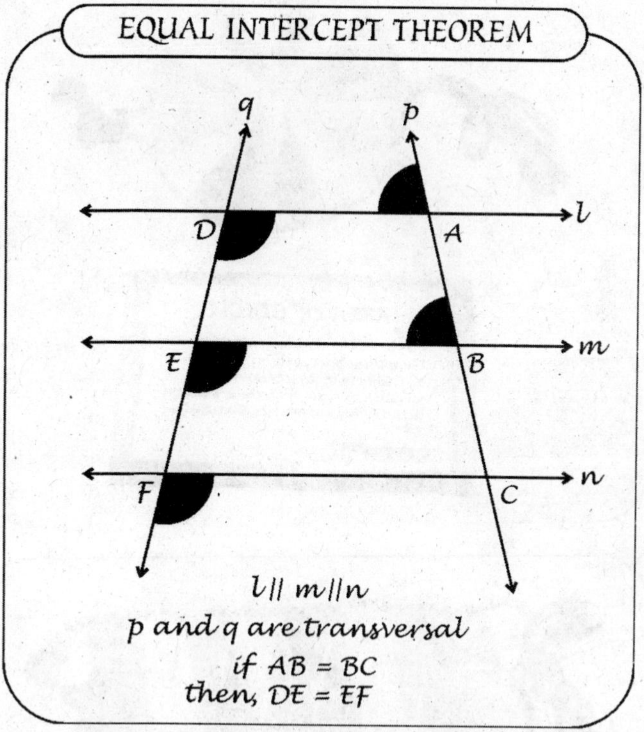

Activity

(i) *Material Required*: Mount board, glazed paper.
(ii) *Description of the Activity*:

This concept can be easily given by the above model. For this draw any line *p*. On it, take three points A, B and C such that AB = BC. Through A, B and C respectively, draw three lines *l*, *m* and *n* parallel to each other. This way have a transversal *p* intersecting three parallel lines *l*, *m* and *n* such that AB = BC. Then, draw another transversal *q* intersecting lines, *l*, *m* and *n* at F, E and D respectively, as shown in the photograph. Now ask the students to measure the intercept EF and DE and observe the result.

7.29 Area of a Circle

Rule: Area of a Circle = πr^2

Activity

(i) *Material Required*: Card board, wool thread.
(ii) *Description of the Activity*:

The concept of the area of a circle can be easily taught with the help of the above model. In this model, sixteen parts of a circle are coloured in different colours in such a way that two parts are cut and coloured in the same colour. In two different wool thread eight parts, one from each colour are attached with the help of these parts attached in wool thread, try to make a rectangle, as shown in the photograph. With the help of this model area of a circle can be easily derived by asking related question, like what is the length, breadth and area of this rectangle.

Length of the rectangle = circumference of the half circle = πr
Breadth of the rectangle = radius of the circle = r
Area of the rectangle = length × breadth
Thus, Area of the circle = $\pi r \times r = \pi r^2$

7.30 Area of Rhombus

Rule: Area of the rhombus = ½ $d_1 \times d_2$

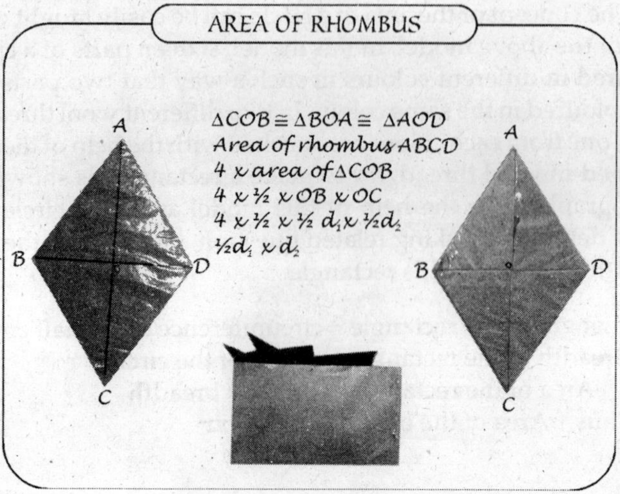

Activity

(i) *Material Required*: Mount board, two rhombus made by card board, one envelop, some right triangles congruent to ΔCOB.

(ii) *Description of the Activity*:

Area of rhombus can easily be taught with the help of this model. In this model, two rhombus made of card board are attached on the mount board and its diagonals are drawn. The diagonals divide the rhombus into four triangles. Also some right triangles, congruent to any one triangle of the rhombus are made and put in the pocket. The students are asked to find out whether four triangles of the rhombus are congruent or not by superimposing the triangle taken from the pocket. With the help of the formula of area of right triangle, students can easily find out the area of rhombus. ΔCOB = ΔBOA = ΔAOD = ΔCOD

$$\begin{aligned}\text{Area of Rhombus ABCD} &= 4 \times \text{area of } \Delta COB \\ &= 4 \times \tfrac{1}{2} \times OB \times OC \\ &= 4 \times \tfrac{1}{2} \times \tfrac{1}{2}d_1 \times \tfrac{1}{2}d_2 \\ &= \tfrac{1}{2} \times d_1 \times d_2\end{aligned}$$

7.31 Surface Area of a Sphere

Rule: Total surface area of the sphere = $4\pi r^2$

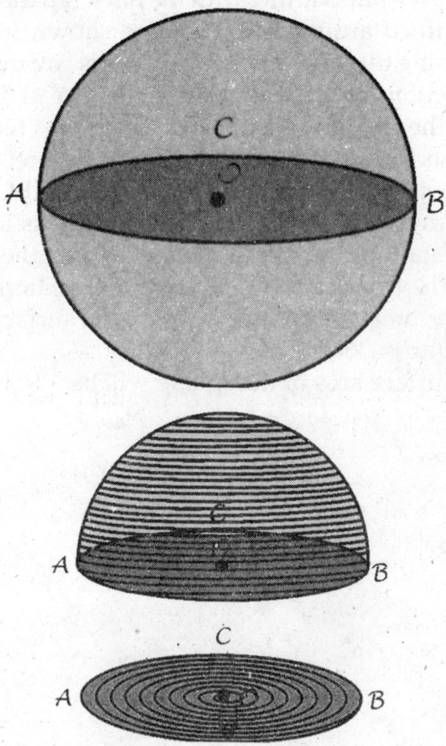

Activity

(i) *Material Required*: Spherical ball, thread, pin and chart paper.

(ii) *Description of the Activity*:

Surface area of a sphere can be easily understood by the following activity:

Take a spherical ball and mark point A, B and C so as to cut the sphere through these points for making two equal halves of the sphere into hemispheres. Cut the sphere by the cutter passing through the centre of the sphere. The base of the hemisphere is a circle named as section ABC with centre O. The centre of this circular section O is the centre of the sphere. Mark the top most point of the hemisphere and fix a pin. Starting with the pin wrap the hemisphere densely with thread around it spirally as shown in the figure. Continue wrapping till the entire hemisphere is covered, that is till we reach the section ABC. Now unwrap the thread and measure its length. Take the circular section ABC separately, fix a pin at the centre O of this section and repeat the wrapping exercise with same thread, starting from its centre till the section ABC is covered completely and unwrap the thread and measure its length. From this we get that length of the thread needed to cover the hemisphere is twice that of the thread needed to cover the section ABC. Since we know that the area of the circle is πr^2, so the surface area of the hemisphere is $2(\pi r^2) = 2\pi r^2$

Thus total surface area of the sphere will be:

$$2(2\pi r^2) = 4\pi r^2$$

7.32 Area of Right Circular Cylinder

Rule: Area of the right circular cylinder = $2\pi r\ (h + r)$

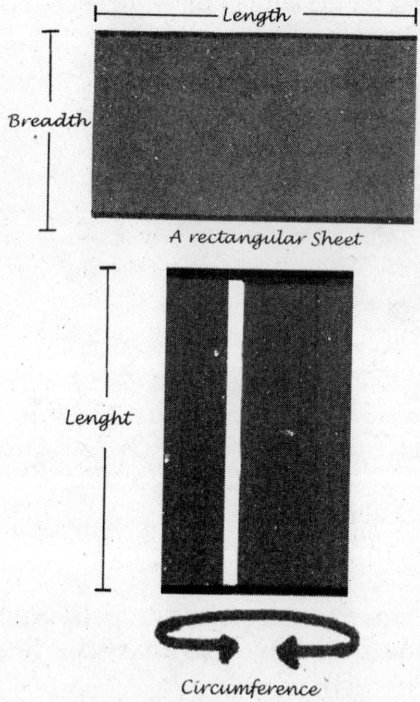

Cylinderical Shape Obtained by Folding the Rectangular Sheet of Paper

NET AREA OF CYLINDER

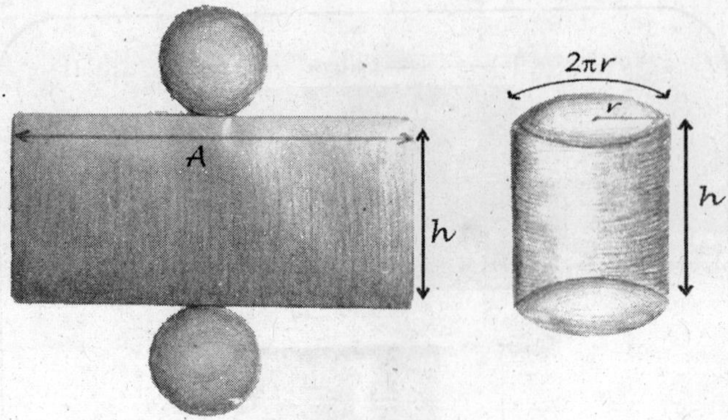

Length of the rectangle sheet (l) $= 2\pi r$

Breadth of the rectangle (b) $= h$

Curved surface area of the cylinder

$= $ Area of the rectangle

$= l \times b$

$= 2\pi r \times h$

$= 2\pi rh$

Total surface area of the cylinder

$=$ Curved surface + area of the base

$= 2\pi rh + 2\pi r^2$

Activity

(i) *Material Required*: A right circular cylinder made of a thick sheet of paper.

(ii) *Description of the Activity*:

Area of a cylinder can be easily taught by the above model. A right circular cylinder made by a thick sheet of paper was used here, as shown in the photograph. After showing the cylinder and discussing different parts of a cylinder the teacher can cut the cylinder along its height with the help of students and open it. Now it becomes a rectangle whose length is same as the circumference of the circle *i.e.*, base and whose breadth is same as the height of the cylinder, as shown in the photograph. Formula of the area of right circular cylinder can be derived by asking different questions *e.g.* what is the length and breadth of this rectangle?

Length of the rectangular sheet = $2\pi r$

Breadth of the rectangular sheet = h

Curved surface area of the cylinder = Area of the rectangle

$$= l \times b$$
$$= 2\pi r \times h$$
$$= 2\pi rh$$

Total surface area of the cylinder = Curved surface area of the cylinder + Area of the two bases

$$= 2\pi rh + 2\pi r^2$$
$$= 2\pi r\,(h + r)$$

7.33 Relationship between the Volumes of Cone and Cylinder

Rule: Volume of the cylinder = 3(volume of the cone with same base radius and height).

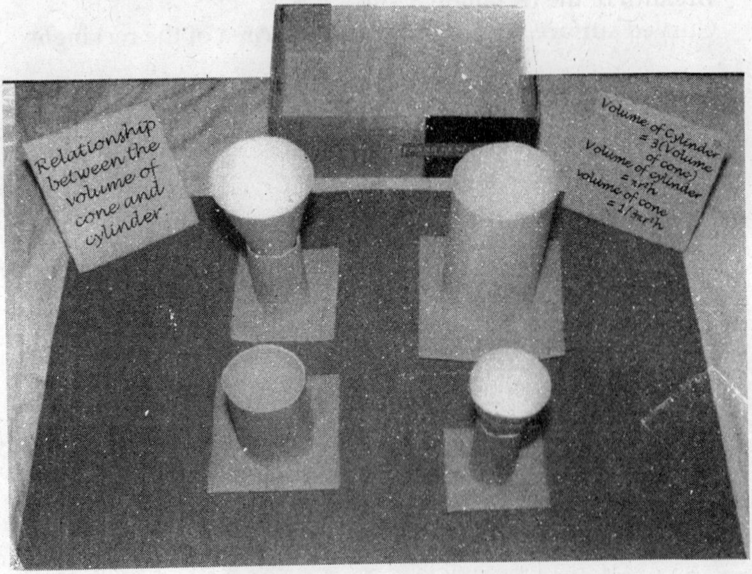

Activity

(i) *Material Required*: Mount board, white sheet, sand or rice.

(ii) *Description of the Activity*:

Making the above model and doing the following activity will help in identifying the relationship between the volumes of cone and cylinder.

With the help of a white sheet, make a cone with height 'h' and radius of the base 'r'. With a similar sheet, make a cylinder with the same height 'h' and the same radius of the base 'r'.

Take some sand and fill the cone with it and pour the sand of the cone into the cylinder. Again fill the cone with sand and pour it into the same cylinder.

It will be found that, the whole cylinder will be filled with three cones of sand.

Thus we get the relationship:

Volume of the cylinder = 3 (volume of the cone with same base radius and height).

7.34 Area of Four Walls of the Room

Rule: Area of four wall = Perimeter of rectangle × height

$$= 2\,(l + b) \times h$$

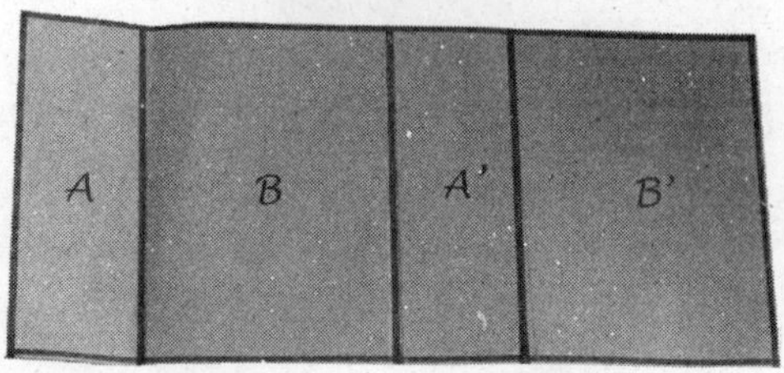

Activity

(i) *Material Required*: A model of a room made by cardboard.

(ii) *Description of the Activity*:

A model of a room made of cardboard can be used to give a better understanding of the concept of area of four walls.

A rectangle with three dotted lines and labelled A, B, A′, B′ is shown to the students, as shown in the figure.

Then a few students are called voluntarily on to the board to perform the activity. The students are told, that since we are concerned with four walls of a room so let us try to fold these dotted lines and notice what will you get?

Teacher then asks the students:

Q. What did you get?

The students replied: A box with four walls A, B, A′ and B′

The teacher again asks the students

Q. What was the original shape of the cardboard?

The students replied: "Rectangle"

The teacher explains that the length of the rectangle is nothing but the perimeter of the room, and the breadth of the rectangle is the height of the room. Hence we can find out the area of the four walls with the help of the following formula:

$$
\begin{aligned}
\text{Area of four walls} &= \text{Area of the rectangle} \\
&= \text{length} \times \text{breadth} \\
&= \text{Perimeter} \times \text{height} \\
&= 2\,(l + b) \times h
\end{aligned}
$$

This is the required formula.

7.35 The Quadratic Equation Solver

Rule: A quadratic equation or a second degree equation is an equation in which highest power of variable is 2.

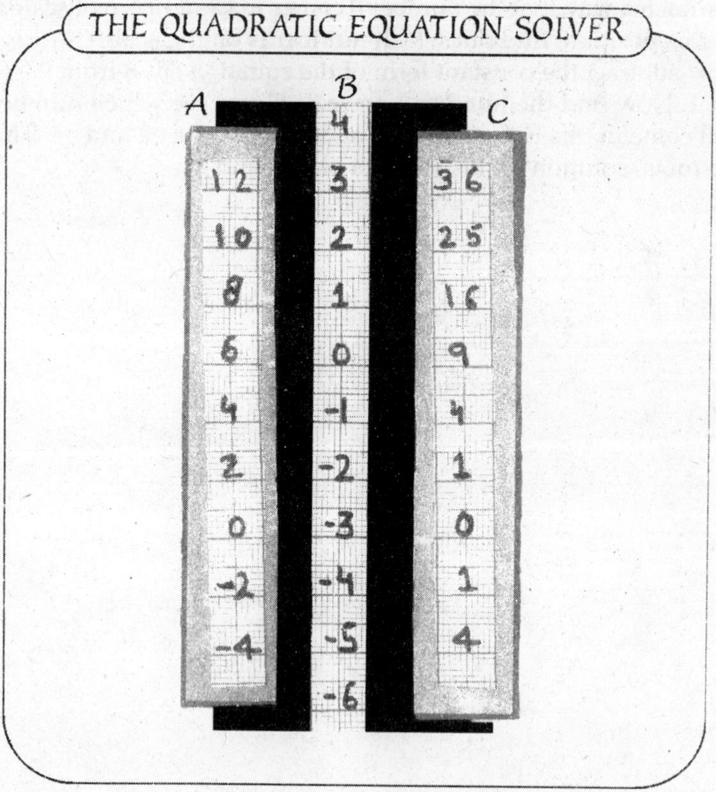

Activity

(i) *Material Required*: Hard board, Graph paper and glaze paper.

(ii) *Description of the Activity*:

This concept is very difficult in it but can be made easy with the help of the above model and activity.

To make this model, take a piece of cardboard, fold it from both the sides, as the panes of a door. Now take another rectangular piece of cardboard and place it between the two folds. Paste a strip of graph paper on the two folds or panes and paste this piece of cardboard such that the centre piece remains movable. Name them as A, B, C as shown in the photograph.

Now to solve an equation (say) $x^2 - 6x + 8 = 0$. Move the scale B in such a way that the number 0 comes in front of + 6 of scale A. At this position, find out which number is on the scale C—it is 9. Now subtract the constant term of the equation *i.e.*, 8 from 9—we get 1. Now find the number 1 on scale C and see which numbers will come in this line on scale A and B which are –2 and –4. Thus the roots/solution of this equation are –2 and –4.

7.36 Parabola

Rule: A parabola is the set of all points in a plane, equidistant from a fixed point and a fixed line in that plane. The fixed point is called the *focus* and the fixed line the *directorix.* The equation $y^2 = 4ax$, $a > 0$ is called the *equation of the parabola*. And each point on the curve satisfies this equation. The chord drawn through the focus and perpendicular to the axis of the parabola is called the *latus rectum*.

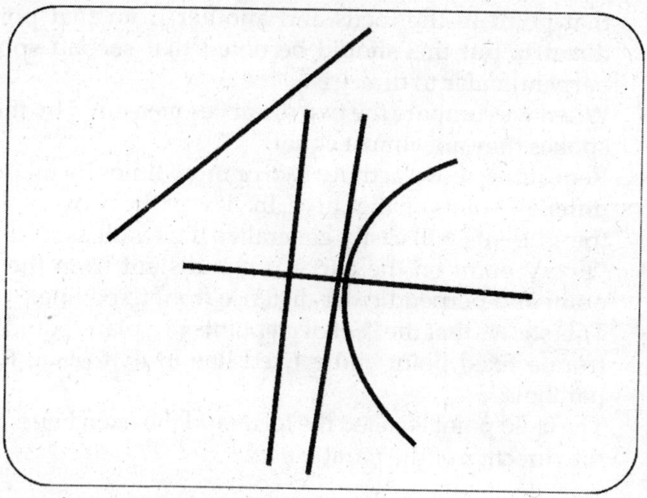

Activity

(i) *Material Required*: A model of parabola made up of iron spokes, two separate spokes.

(ii) *Description of the Activity*:

The concept of parabola, its parts and the derivation of the equation of parabola can be easily given by this model. The given model is made up of iron spokes in which two spokes are joined by their mid-points to form a coordinate axis. We suppose the horizontal line as x-axis and the vertical line as y-axis. Another spoke is joined on the negative sides of the X-axis at some distance from the origin of the parabola to Y-axis and this becomes the directrix of the parabola. On the right side a curve is placed in such a way that its mid- point is at origin (we later generalize that it is a parabola). Also on positive direction of X-axis a point is marked such that its distance from origin is equal to the distance of the directrix from origin. Then this point becomes be the focus of the parabola.

There are two other spokes also which we use to measure the distance of any point on the curve to the directrix and the focus.

The working rule of the given model is as follows:

- First of all make a point on the curve, place one spoke from that point to the focus and another from that point to directrix but this should be noted that second spoke is perpendicular to directrix.
- When we compare the two distances measured by the two spokes they are almost equal.
- Repeat the above activity two or more times by taking the different points on the curve. In view of the above activities the students will easily generalize the result as.
- "Every point on the curve is equidistant from the fixed point and perpendicular distance from fixed line."
- This shows that the "Set of all points in a plane equidistant from a fixed point and a fixed line in that plane form a parabola".
- The fixed point is called the focus and the fixed line is called the directrix of the parabola.

The distance PF is given by

$$PF = \sqrt{(x-a)^2 + (y-0)^2}$$

$$= \sqrt{(x-a)^2 + y^2}$$

The distance from P to the line L is

$$d = |x+a|$$

Since PF = d, we have

or $\quad (x-a)^2 + y^2 = |x+a|^2 = (x+a)^2$

or $\quad x^2 - 2ax + a^2 + y^2 = x^2 + 2ax + a^2$

or $\quad y^2 = 4ax, \; a > 0 \qquad$ (i)

The equation (i) is called the equation of the parabola. And each point on the curve satisfies equation (i)

The chord drawn through the focus and perpendicular to the axis of the parabola is called the latus rectum.

7.37 Match the Formulae

Rule: Different formulae

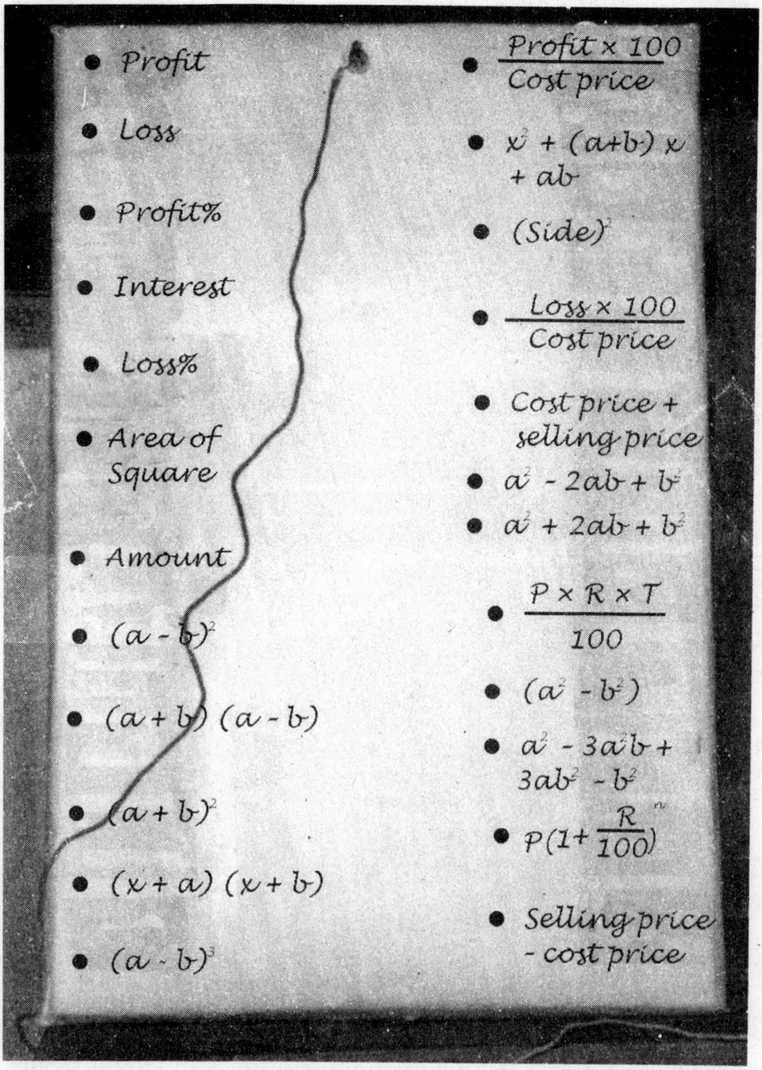

Activity

(i) *Material Required*: Wooden board, small bulb, electric wires.

(ii) *Description of the activity*:

A model can be made up in the form of a game, in which formulae are written in one column and the names of the formulae are written in the other column. Students are asked to match the formulae and their names. If the answer is correct only then the light will glow, otherwise it will not.

7.38 Formula Wheel

Rule: Perimeter and area of different geometrical figures.

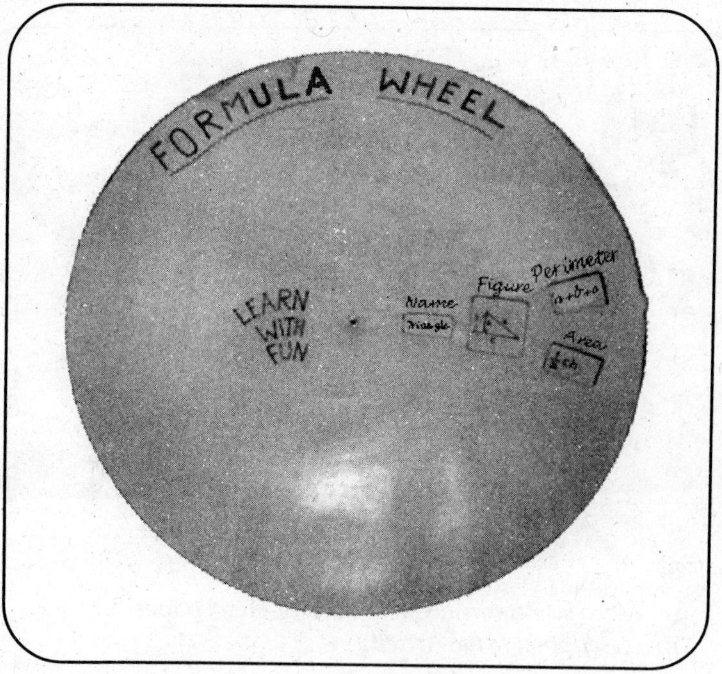

Activity

(i) *Material Required*: Two wheels made of cardboard, screw.

(ii) *Descripticn of the Activity*:

In this model there are two wheels made of cardboard joined at the centre with the help of a screw. One of them has four windows (cut outs) labelled as—'Name' (of the figure), 'Figure', 'Perimeter' and 'Area', as shown in the picture. The other wheel has the names of different figures, their shapes, respective perimeters and areas written on it.

By rotating the wheel, we get different figures under the windows and accordingly their name, perimeter and area respectively. In this way, names of different figures, their shapes, respective perimeter and areas can easily be taught.

7.39 Indian Mathematician

Rule: Important contributions of Indian mathematicians.

Activity

(i) *Material Required*: Cardboard or chart paper.
(ii) *Description of the Activity*

Important contribution of our mathematicians can be displayed in a beautiful and interesting manner that can attract students to read it.

8

Charts

8.1 Introduction

Charts are one of the most commonly used teaching aids. Charts are a systematic arrangement of key facts or ideas in a logical sequence or representing ideas and facts in a pictorial or graphical form. They help in creating a suitable subject atmosphere in the classroom and in elucidating various points. It is an effective medium in mathematics teaching. Almost all mathematical concepts can be illustrated with pictures, which can even take a place of concrete manipulative. For example, if you can condition your child to draw lots of apple pictures when studying fractions, he/she can learn to visualize fractions as 'apples'. Then he/she won't make the addition mistake like $1/2 + 1/4 = 3/4$. Charts are the best ways for pictorial representation of concepts.

They save the teachers' time, as in place of drawing figures in the class, teachers can use figures already made on the chart. The charts can be used for variety of purposes such as:

- Depicting various geometrical figures and their properties.
- Comparing properties of different geometrical figures.
- Highlighting key points in a lesson.
- Concretizing abstract mathematical concepts into visual forms.
- Summarizing a lesson.
- Showing the sequence of steps in geometrical constructions.
- Charts can be prepared for various units of length and weight. Relationships among the various units of measurement can be easily illustrated with the help of a chart.

- Depicting certain important formulae or results of mathematics *e.g.*

$$S.I. = \frac{P \times R \times T}{100}$$

Area of a rectangle = length × breadth
Area of circle = $2\pi r$ and so on.

- Introducing a lesson (some activity based chart to check the previous knowledge can be used.)

Some concepts, which can be easily taught with the help of charts, are as follows:

8.2 Definition of Mathematics

Mathematics can be defined in a number of ways, children defined it in different manner whereas adults have a different way to define it. Two separate charts can be displayed for this purpose, as shown in photograph.

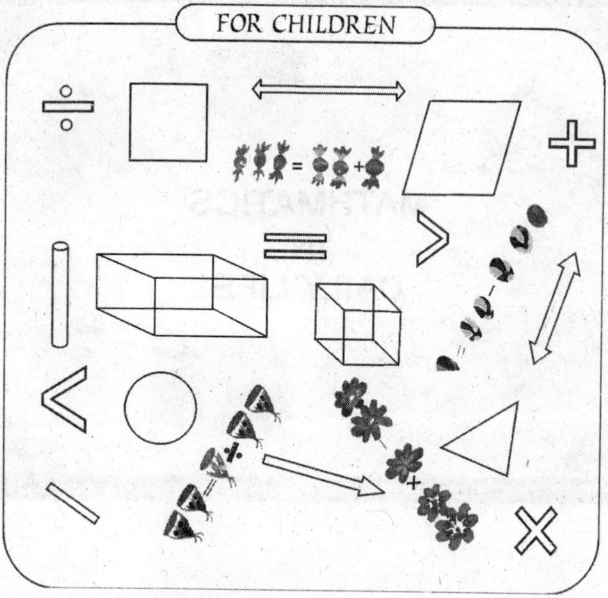

FOR ADULT

Mathematics is the science of numbers and space.

Mathematics is the science of measurement, quantity and magnitude.

Mathematics is the science in which calculation are prime.

Mathematics is a science of logical reasoning.

Mathematics has its own language. This language consists mathematical terms, mathematical concepts and formulae.

8.3 Uses of Mathematics

As we discussed earlier that mathematics is used in every walk of life. Drawings to depict various uses of mathematics in daily life can be displayed on a bulletin board.

8.4 Angle Made by a Transversal in Two Parallel Lines

The relationship between the angles made by a transversal on two parallel lines can be depicted with the help of charts by showing different kinds of angles with different colours. e.g., all the corresponding angles with red colour, all alternate angles with green colours etc.

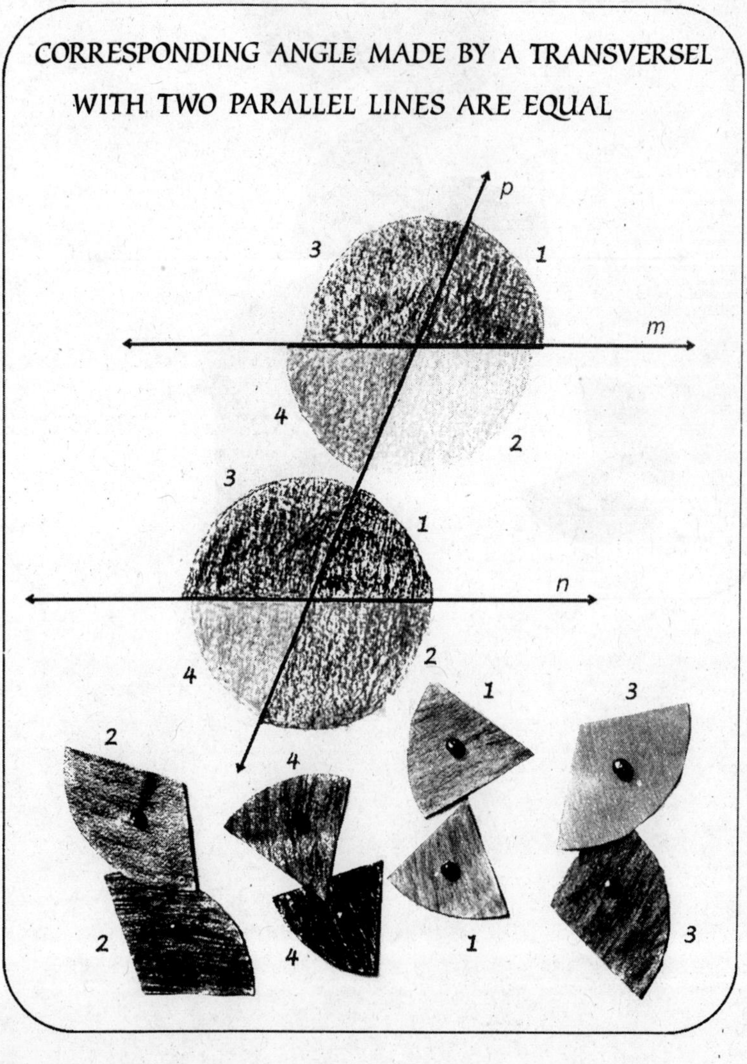

INTERIOR ALTERNATE ANGLE OF TRANSFERAL AND TWO PARALLEL LINES ARE EQUAL

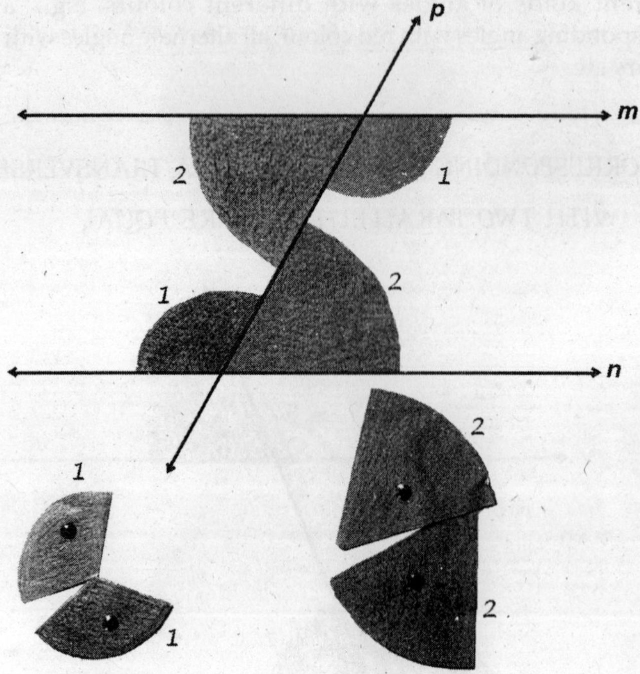

8.5 Equal Intercept Property

Equal intercept property can be depicted on a chart as follows:

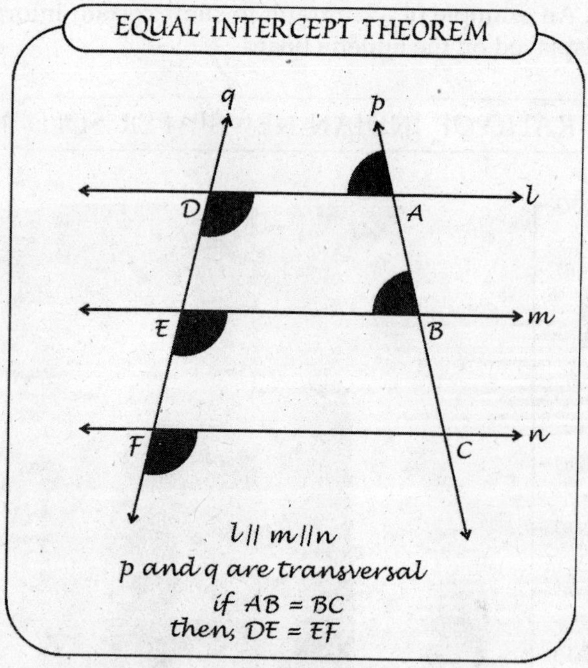

8.6 Bar Graph

Bar graph is a very useful device to represent a data in a concise way. We can infer a lot of informations about the data simply by seeing it. An example of a bargraph to show certain information can be displayed on the bulletin board.

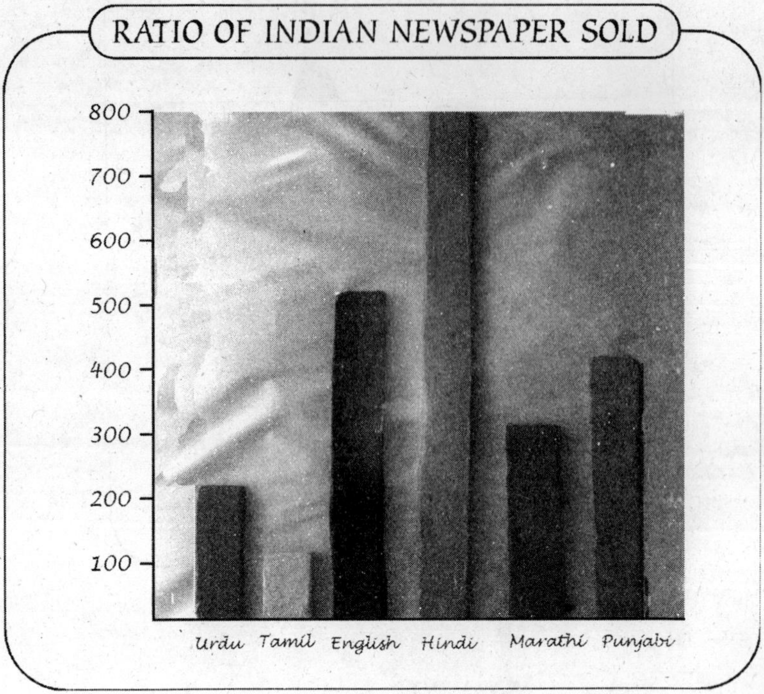

8.7 Properties of Triangle

Different properties of triangles can be easily verified with the help of charts e.g., 'sum of any two sides of a triangle is greater than the third side' can be verified by the activity shown in the following chart.

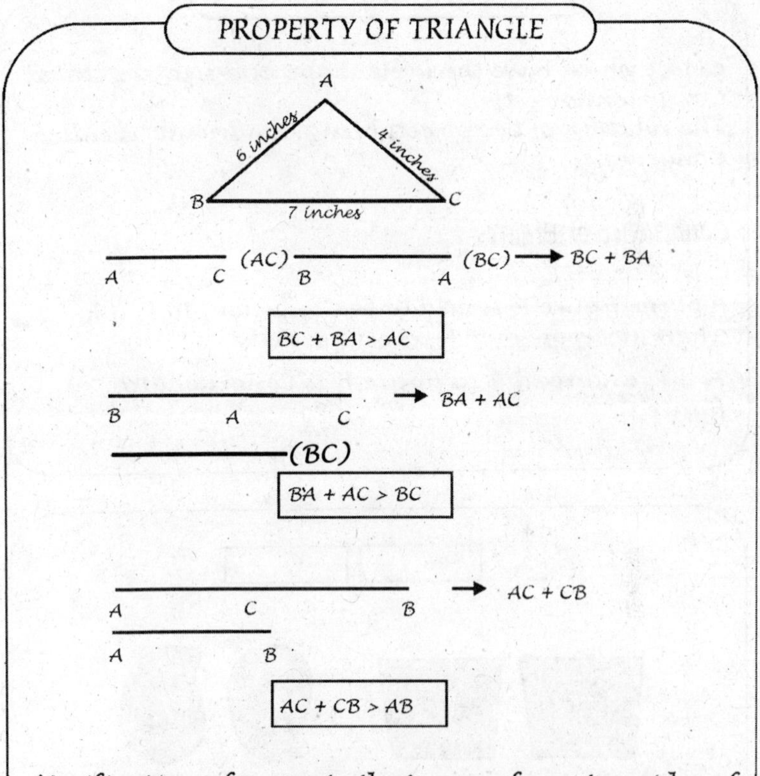

Verification of property that, sum of any two sides of a Δ is greater than that of the third side.

8.8 Concept of Congruence

Concept of congruence occupies a very important place in geometry. Definition of congruence with the help of different examples can be displayed on charts.

CONGRUENCE

Object which have the same shape and size are called Congruent objects.
The relation of two objects being Congruent is called Congruence.

Congruence of Figures

A plane figure F_1 is said to be Congruent to F_2 if F_1 when superpose over F_2 cover it exactly.

$F_1 \cong F_2$ and read it as figure F_1 is Congruent to figure F_2.

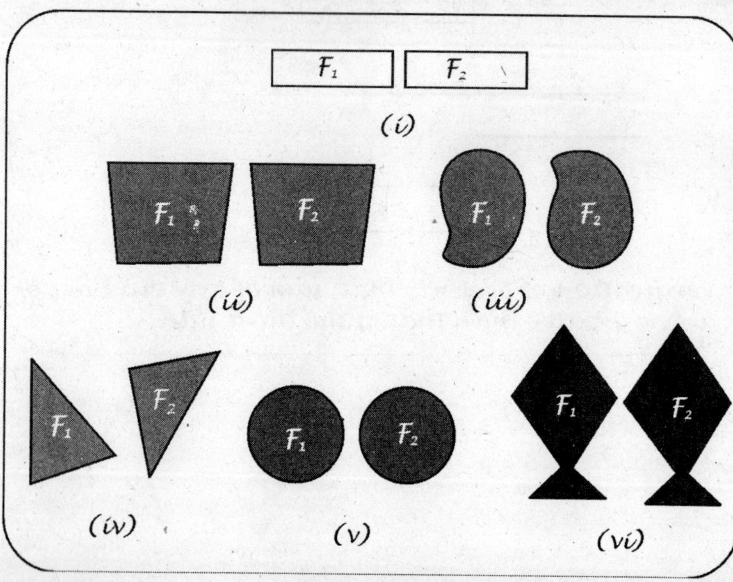

CONGRUENCE OF FIGURE

Identify the pair of congruent figure.

8.9 Criteria for the Congruence of Triangles

Different criteria for the congruence of triangles such as ASA, SAS & RHS can easily be depicted on a chart.

IDENTIFY THE CRITERIA OF CONGRUENCE

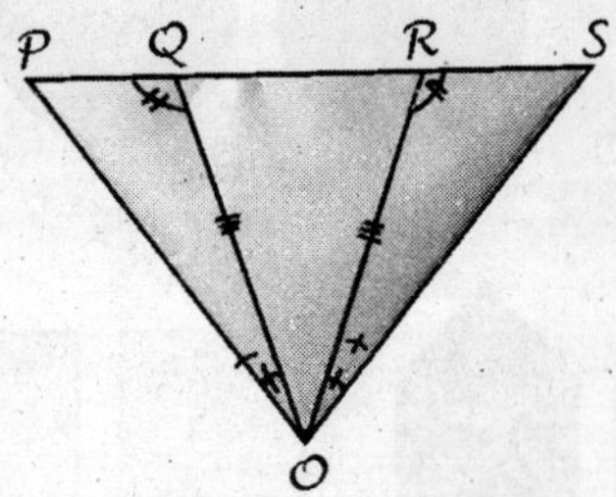

$\angle POQ = \angle SOR$
$\angle OQP = \angle ORS$
$QO = RO$
$\triangle OPQ \cong \triangle OSR$

ASA

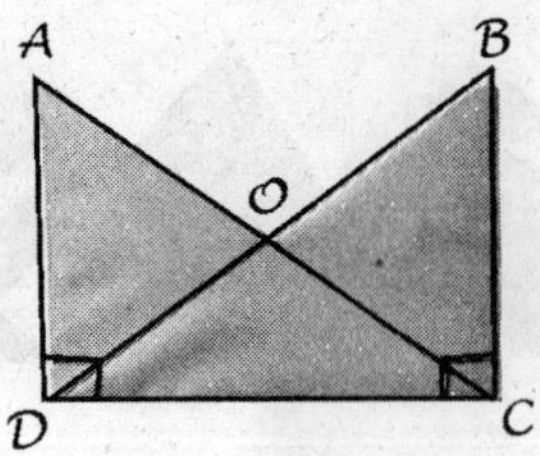

$\angle ADC = \angle BCD = 90^\circ$
$AC = BD$
$\triangle ADC \cong \triangle BCD$

RHS

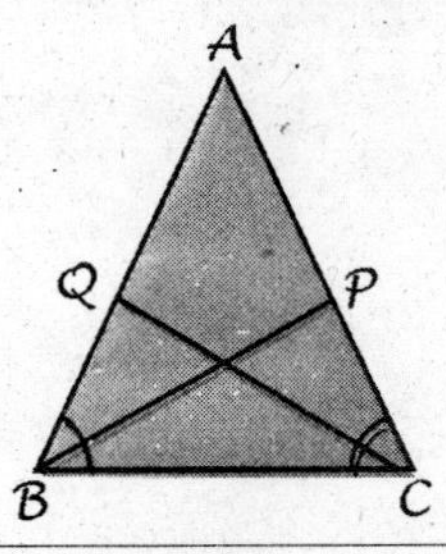

$\angle ABC = \angle ACB$
$QB = PC$
$\triangle QBC \cong \triangle PBC$

SAS

8.10 Construction of Triangles

How can we construct two congruent triangles? Different instructions to construct two congruent triangles can be displayed on charts while teaching this concept.

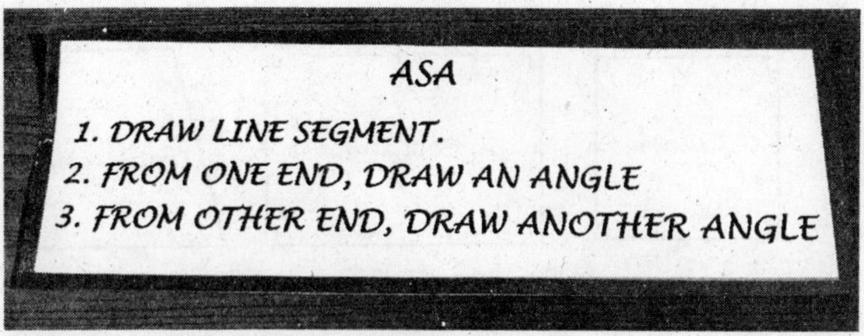

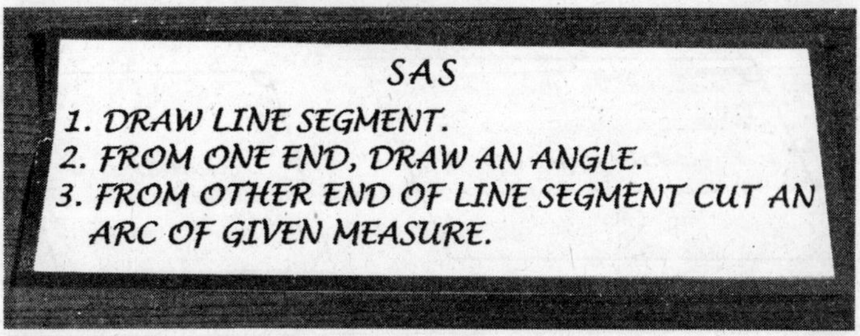

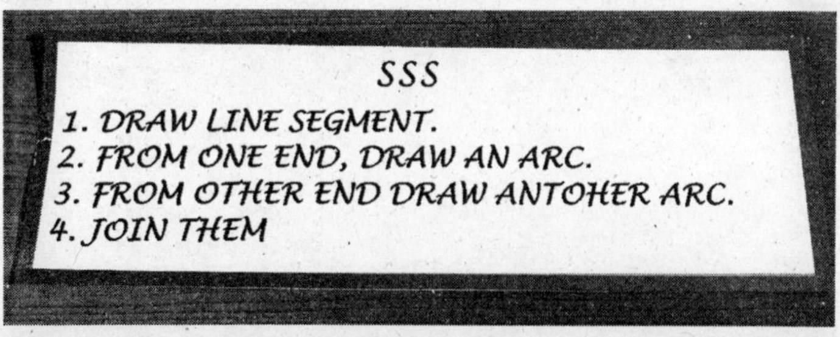

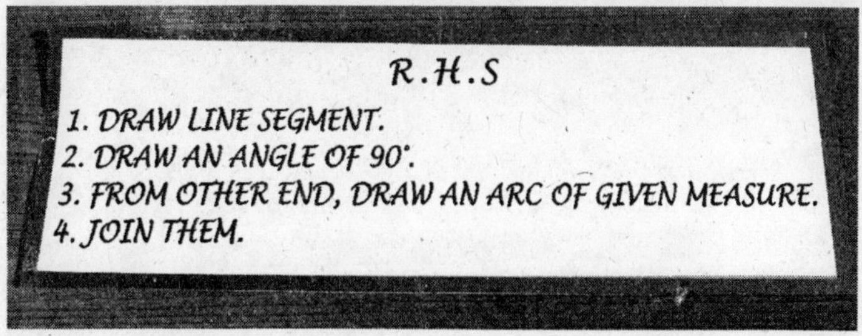

8.11 Different Types of Quadrilaterals

Cutouts of different types of quadrilaterals can be displayed, a chart.

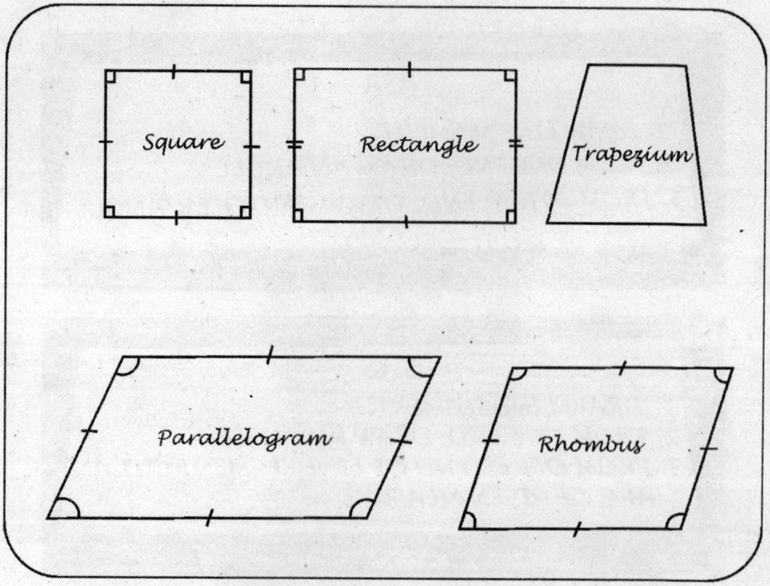

8.12 Area of Trapezium

An activity to find the area of trapezium can be displayed on a chart.

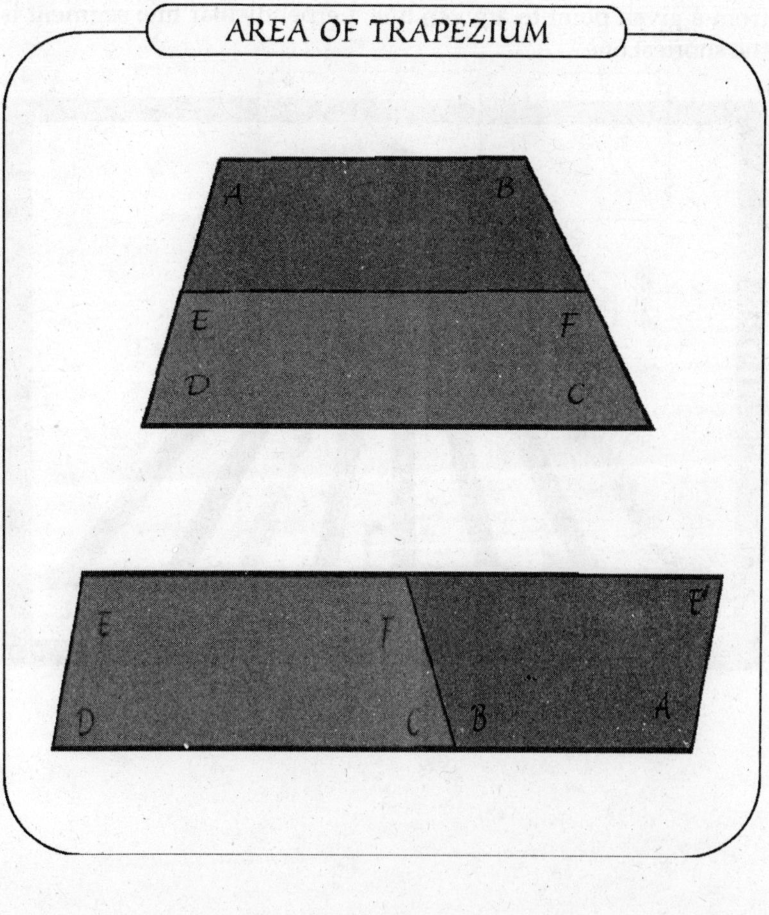

8.13 Among all the line segments drawn from a given point to a given line, perpendicular line segment is the shortest

Different coloured tapes can be used to give an attractive appearance of the property that, "among all the live segments drawn from a given point to a given line, perpendicular line segment is the shortest one.

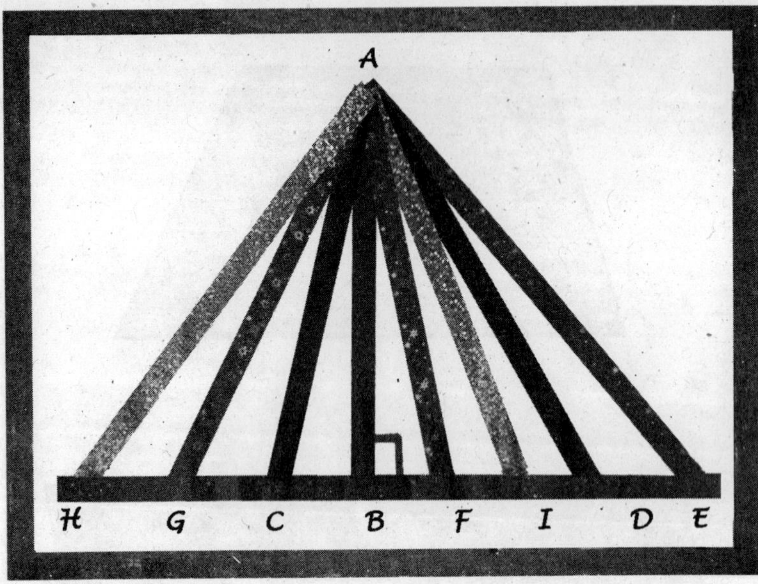

8.14 In a Circle Perpendicular from the Centre to a Chord Bisects the Chord

An activity to verify the property that, in a circle, perpendicular from the centre to a chord, bisects the chord, can be shown on a chart by giving the steps of activity and the figure obtained by following these steps, as shown in the following chart.

ACTIVITY

STEP 1

TAKE THE CIRCEL MADE OF PAPER AND MARK CENTRE 'O'.

STEP 2

COVER THE CIRCLE OVER ITSELF.

STEP 3

FOLD THE CIRCLE FROM ONE OF ITS SIDE AS SHOWN.

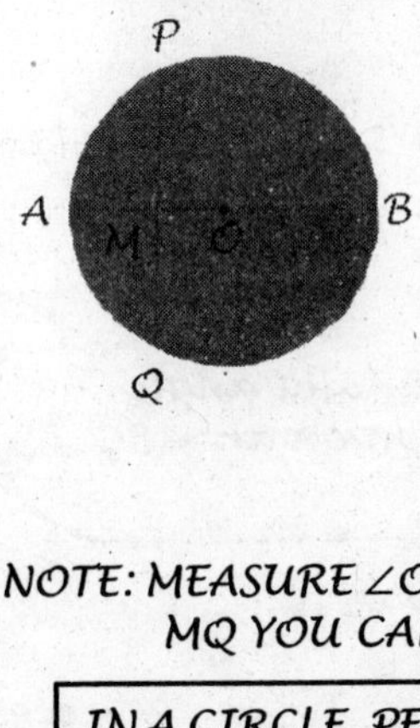

STEP 4

UNFOLD THE CIRCLE MADE BY PAPER DRAW THE LINES PQ AND AB ON THE IMPRESSIONS AS SHOWN. ALSO MARK CENTRE 'O' OF CIRCLE POINT OF INTERSECTION OF AB < PQ IS 'M'.

NOTE: MEASURE $\angle OMQ$ AND $\angle OMP$ AND LENGTH PM AND MQ YOU CAN OBSERVE:

IN A CIRCLE, PERPENDICULAR FROM THE CENTER TO A CHORD, BISECTS THE CHORD.

8.15 Angle Properties of a Circle

Properties of angles relating to circles can be shown on charts as follows:

ANGLE PROPERTIES IN A CIRCLE

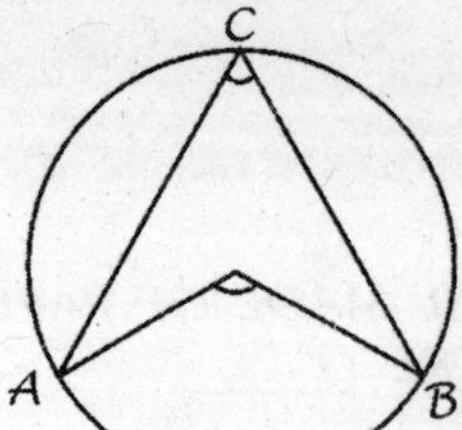

CIRCLE

The angle subtended by an Arc at the center, is double the Angle subtended by it at any Point on the remaining part of the circle.

∠ABC = ½ ∠ADC

∠ADC = 2 ∠ABC

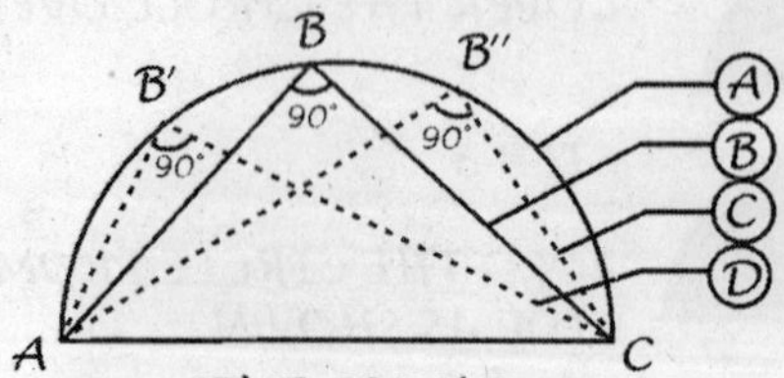

SEMI CIRCLE

THE ANGLE IN A SEMI CIRCLE IS ALWAYS A RIGHT ANGLE.

A = Arc ABC
B = Right angle ABC
C = B & B'' are point on arc ABC
d = AC is a diameter of semi circle Right angle AB'C & AB''C at different position on arc ABC in a semi circle.

PROPERTIES OF ANGLES RELATING TO CIRCLES

Angle in a semicircle is right angle.

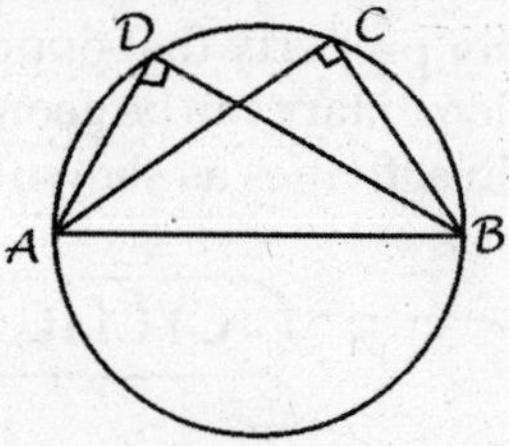

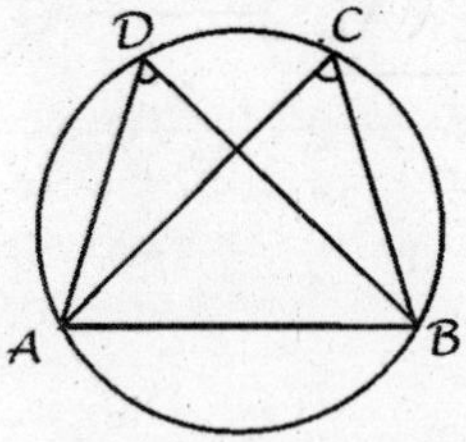

Angles in the same segment are equal

8.16 Cyclic Quadrilateral and Its Angles

Definition of Cyclic quadrilateral, its angle sum property and its another property that opposite angles of a cyclic quadrilateral are supplementary can be geometrically proved on charts by following certain activities as shown in the charts given below:

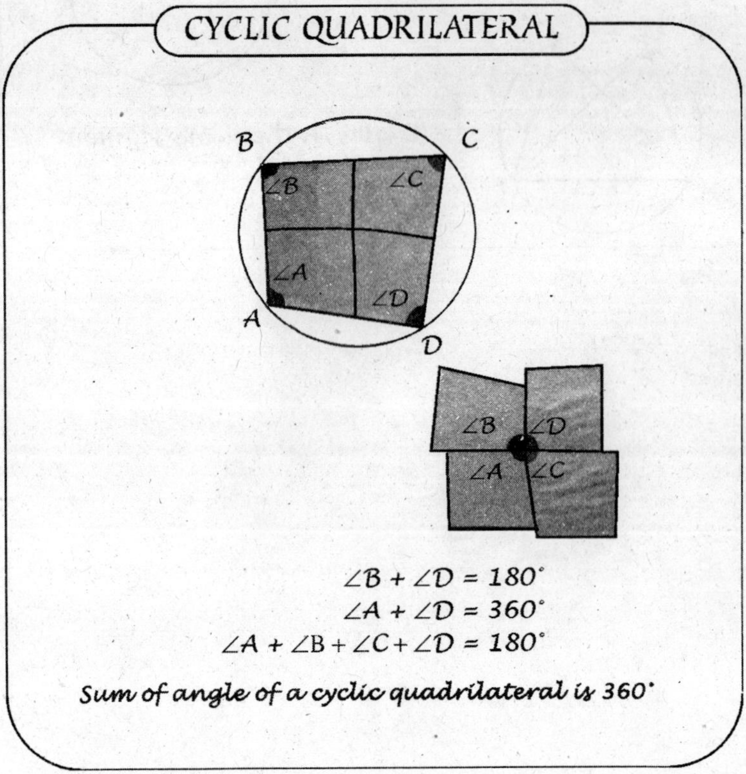

GEOMETRICAL PROOF OF THE PROPERTY THAT OPPOSITE ANGLE OF A CYCLIC QUADRILATERAL ARE SUPPLEMENTARY

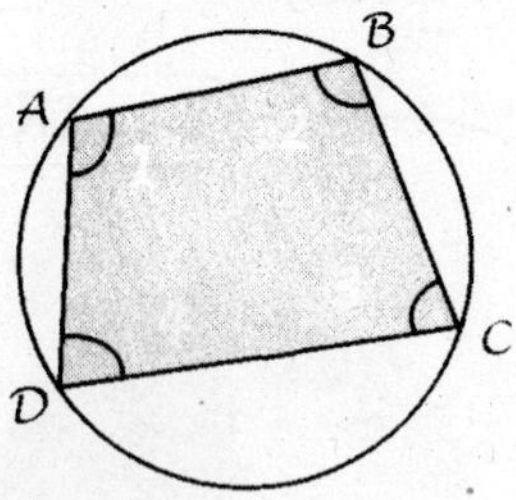

1. Take the adjoining figure, here ABCD is a cyclic quadrilateral.
2. Cut the four angle 1, 2, 3, 4.
3. Place the angles 1 and 3 as below.
4. Place the angles 2 and 4 as below.

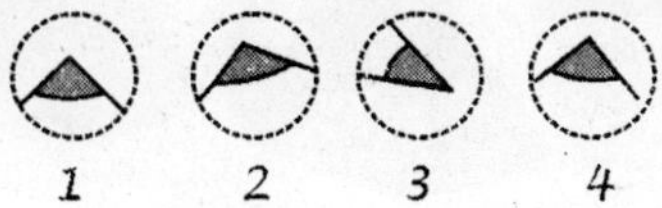

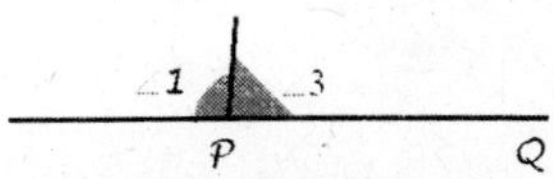

From above activity, we can conclude

$\angle 1 + \angle 3 = 180^\circ$

[Linear pair]

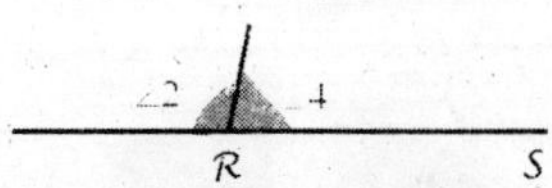

From above activity, we can conclude

$\angle 2 + \angle 4 = 180^\circ$

[Linear pair]

Hence we can generate that:

Opposite angles of cyclic quadrilateral are supplementary.

8.17 Area of Circle

An activity to find the area of a circle can be effectively shown on a chart as follows:

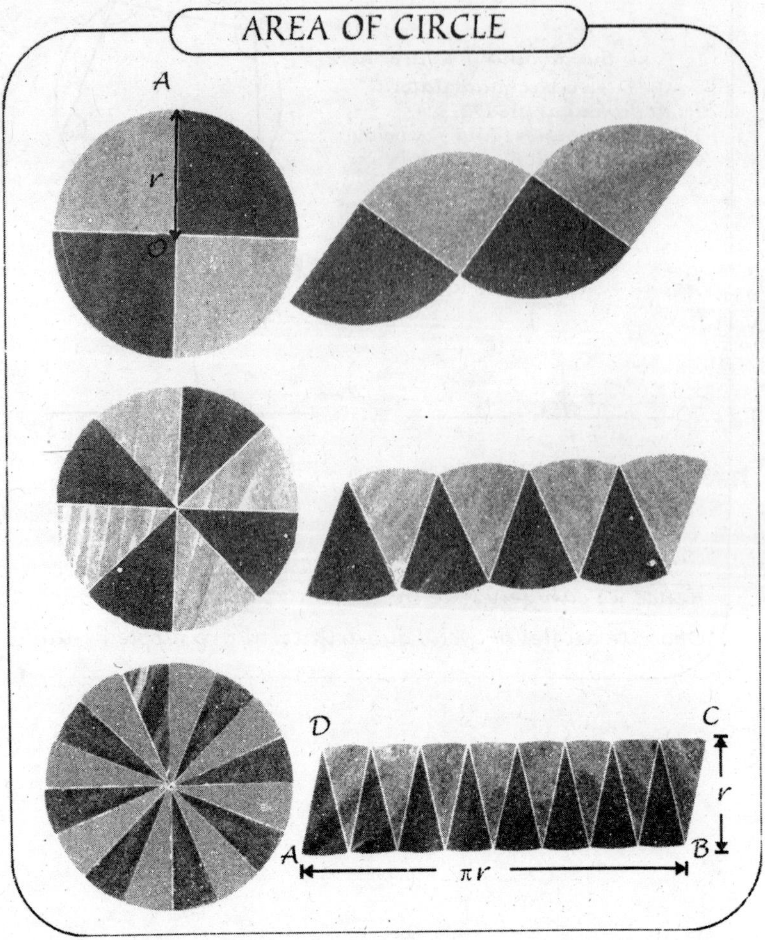

8.18 Pythagoras Theorem

Squares of different sizes made by cardboard can be arranged on a chart to verify the Pythagoras theorem, as follows:

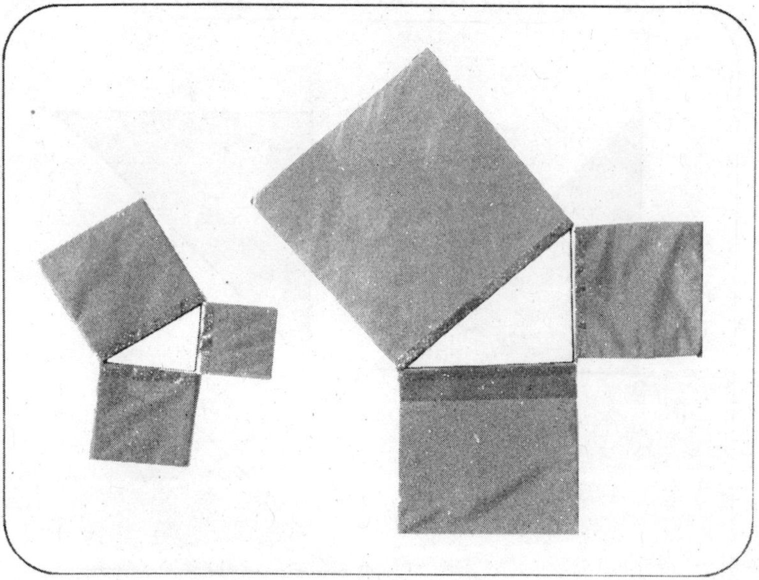

Pythagorous theorem can also be verified by an activity depicted on a chart as follows:

PYTHAGORAS THEOREM

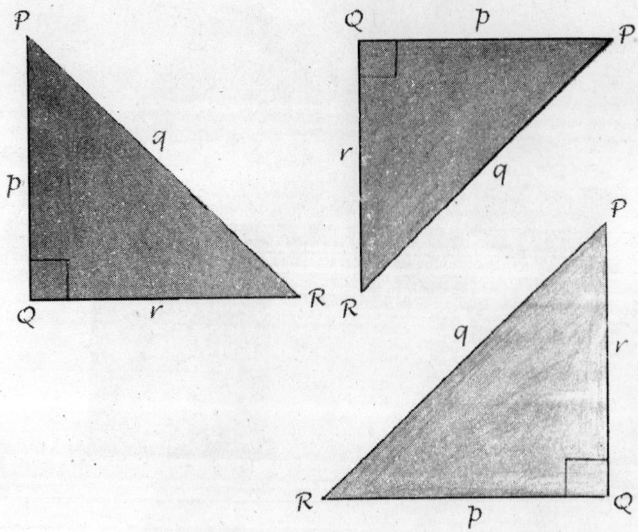

Right Triangle	Measurement			Square				Difference
	p	r	q	p^2	r^2	q^2	$p^2 + r^2$	$q^2 - (p^2 + r^2)$
1.								
2.								
3.								

The difference $q^2 - (p^2 + r^2)$, in each case is either 0 or so small that the same may be treated as zero.

$\therefore q^2 = (p^2 + r^2)$

This activity illustrates the following proposition. In the right triangle, the square of the hypotenuse equals the sum of square of its sides.

8.19 Area of Path

If a child can imagine the right shape of a figure then he can easily find out its area by applying different formulae, he has already studied. Same thing can be done in the case of finding the area of path. To give the right image of paths, different charts can be used.

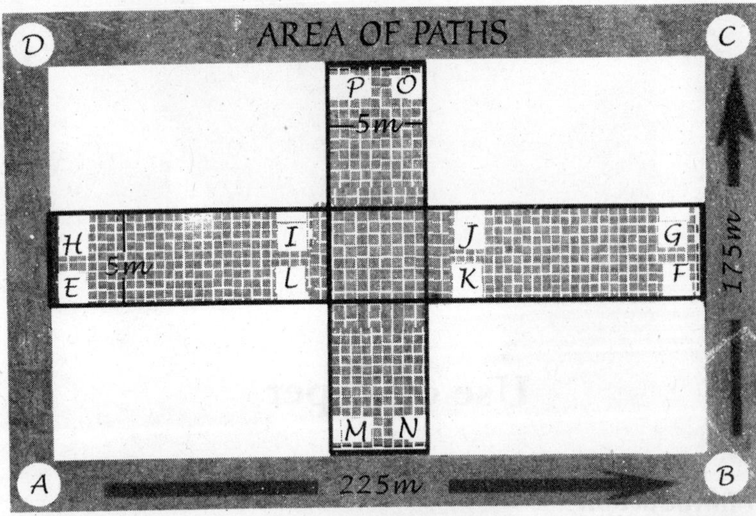

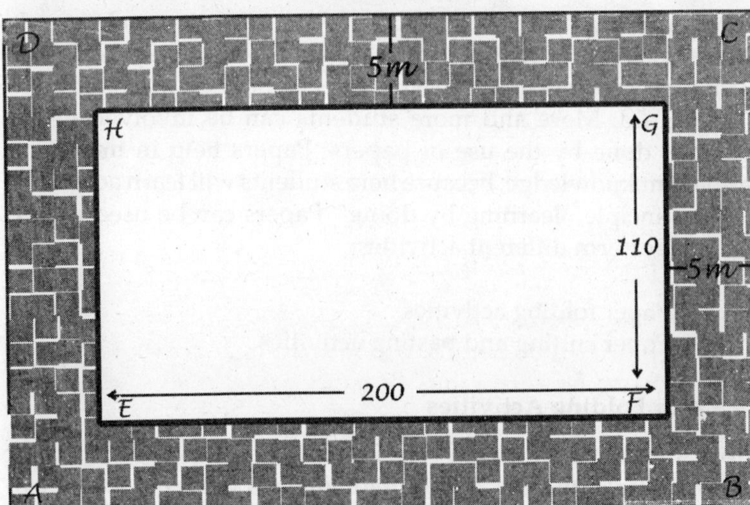

9

Use of Paper

9.1 Introduction

Money and time both are used in making effective teaching aids for the teaching of mathematics. But pieces of papers are easily available in the classroom itself. They can be used as an effective teaching aid. More and more students can be involved in the activities done by the use of papers. Papers help in imparting permanent knowledge, because here students will learn according to the principle, 'learning by doing'. Papers can be used in two ways to perform different activities:

- Paper folding activities.
- Paper cutting and pasting activities.

9.2 Paper Folding Activities

Paper folding activities are very helpful to teach some important mathematical concepts. Some mathematical concepts which can be taught through paper folding activities are as follows:

9.2.1 Concept of Fraction

Rule: Fraction can be defined as 'a part of a whole' or 'a part of a group'.

$\frac{1}{2}$ $\frac{1}{3}$ $\frac{1}{4}$

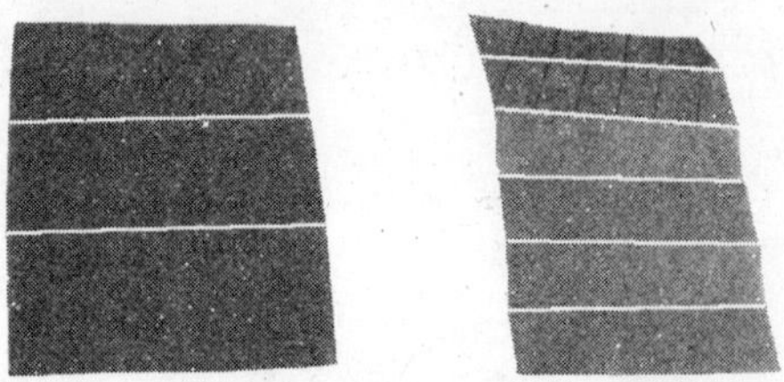

$\frac{1}{3}$ $\frac{2}{6}$

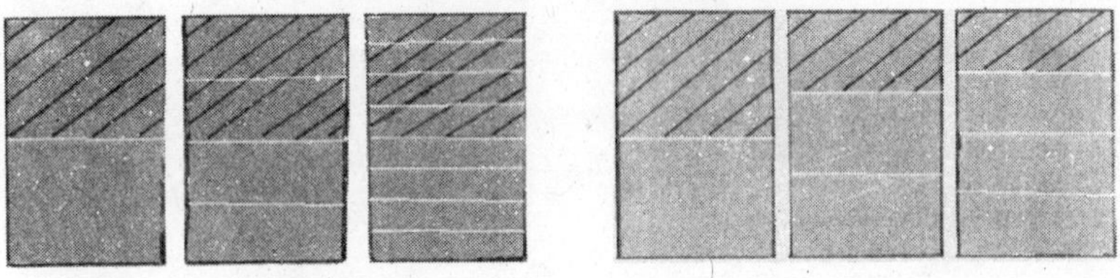

$\frac{1}{2}$ $\frac{2}{4}$ $\frac{4}{8}$ $\frac{1}{2}$ $\frac{1}{3}$ $\frac{1}{4}$

Activity

(i) *Material Required*: Sheet of paper.

(ii) *Description of the Activity*:

Concept of fractions can easily be taught by paper folding activity. Teacher can give a piece of paper in rectangular shape to each student and ask them to fold it into two, three or four equal parts and then shade one part and tell the students that, this shaded portion represents the 1/2, 1/3 or 1/4 part. By repeating this activity in different ways the students get the concept of fraction.

After this, teacher can give another piece of same size and shape. Ask them to fold it four, six or eight times and open it, now shade two portions. By comparing of these two pieces of 1/3 and 2/6 students can observe that 1/3 and 2/6 represent the same portion of the paper. Hence they are equivalent. By repeating this activity, and folding the paper nine times, twelve times, fifteen times and so on. The students get the concept of equivalent fractions *i.e.* 1/3 = 2/6 = 3/9 = 4/12 = 5/15. Similarly by comparing 1/2, 2/4 and 4/8 fractions students get the concept that they are also equal.

9.2. 2 Concept of Exponents

Rule: Exponents represent number of times a number is multiplied *e.g.*,

$$\chi^{\text{ਅ}} = \chi \times \chi \times \chi \ldots\ldots \chi (\text{ਅ ਵਜਠ ਕਤ})$$

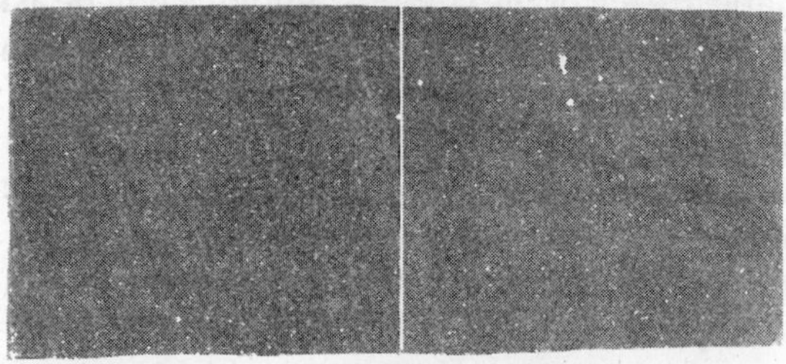

Fold I

Fold II

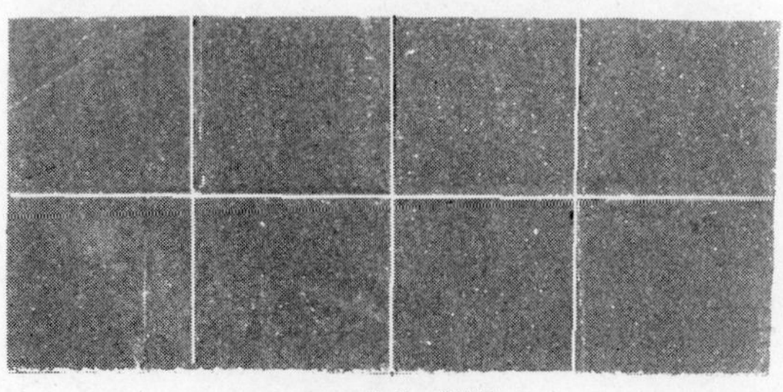

Fold III

Activity:

(i) *Material Required*: Sheet of paper.
(ii) *Description of the Activity*:

Concept of exponents can easily be given by paper folding activity.

- For this teacher will give a sheet of paper in rectangular shape to each of the student. Students will be asked to fold this rectangle into two equivalent parts, press the fold and then open it and count the parts.
- Now again fold the paper, press it, open it and count the parts, again fold it, press it, open it and count the parts and so on.
- Students can easily be observed that in first fold there are two equivalent parts which represent $2 = 2$, in second fold there are four equivalent parts which represent $2^2 = 4$, in the third fold there are eight equivalent parts which represent $2^3 = 8$ and so on. Here number of folds represents exponent of 2 and the number of parts represent its value.

By this activity exponents of 3, 4, 5 ... can also be taught by folding the sheet in 3, 4, 5 ... times at a time.

9.2.3 Concept of Factorization of Algebraic Expression

Rule: Factorization of Algebraic Expression means, breaking of the algebraic expression into its constituent parts in such a way that when we multiply these parts, we get that expression again.

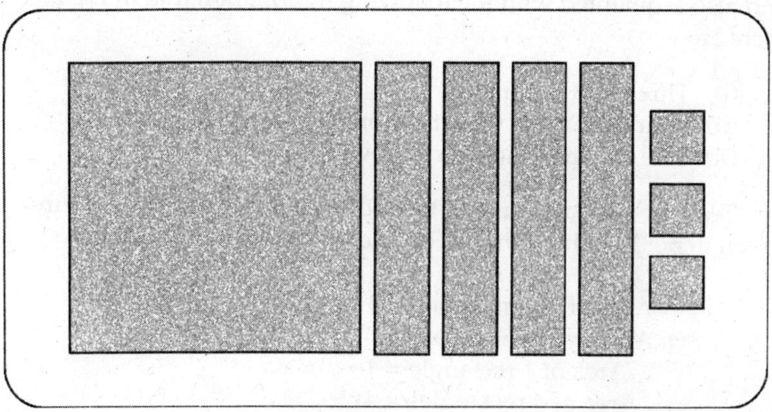

Box A

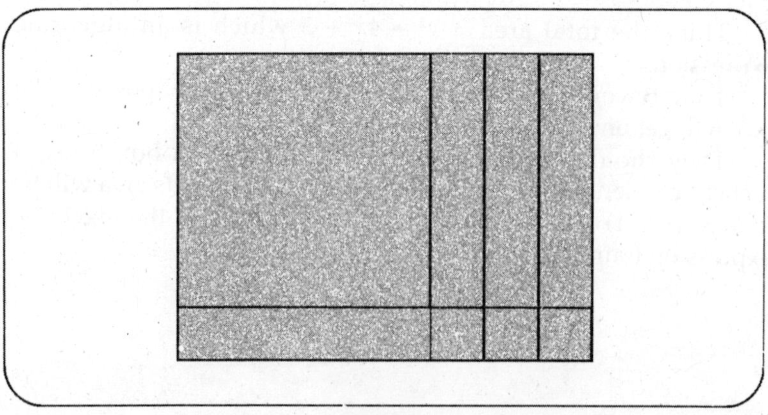

Box B

Activity

(i) *Material Required*: Sheet of paper.

(ii) *Description of the Activity:*

Concept of Factorization of Algebraic Expression can be easily taught by the following activity:

The whole class would be divided into 2 groups i.e., team A and team B. Both the teams would be given the figures as given in box A and also acquainted with the following information that in the box there are—

(i) Three unit squares.
(ii) Four rectangles which are one unit wide and x-unit long.
(ii) One square which is x-unit wide.

Team A would be asked to find the area of all these figures given in box A, which should be like this.

$$\begin{aligned} &\text{Area of 1 unit square} = 1\\ \therefore\ &\text{Area of 3 unit square} = 3\\ &\text{Area of 1 rectangle} = 1 \times x = x\\ \therefore\ &\text{Area of 4 rectangles} = 4x\\ &\text{Area of x-unit square} = x^2 \end{aligned}$$

Thus, the total area = $x^2 + 4x + 3$ which is an algebraic expression.

Team B would be asked to try to join all these shapes given in box A to get one figure & find its area.

They should get the shape which is given in box B i.e., a rectangle of length $x + 3$ and of breadth $x + 1$. Thus its area will be $(x + 3)\ (x + 1)$ which is nothing but the factors of the algebraic expression found by team A. i.e.,

$$x^2 + 4x + 3 = (x + 1)\ (x + 3)$$

9.2.4. Concept of Different Geometrical Shapes

Rule: Different geometrical figures are triangles, square, rectangle, parallelogram, rhombus, perpendicular to a line, bisector of an angle.

Perpendicular to a line

Bisector of an Angle

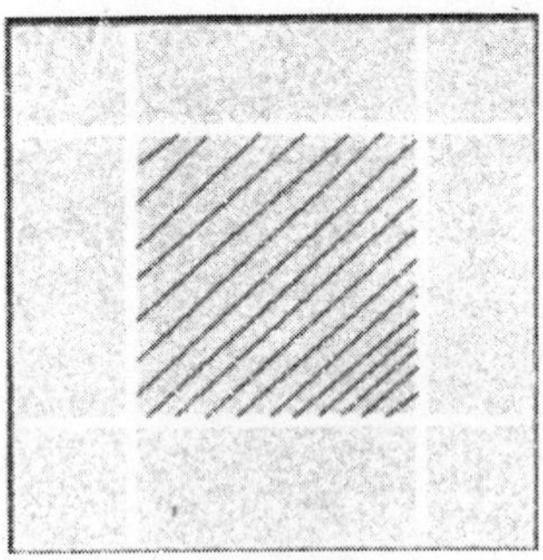

Square

Rectangle

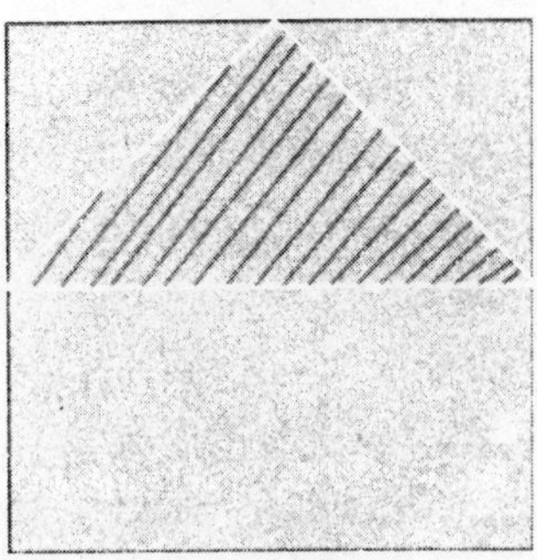

Triangle

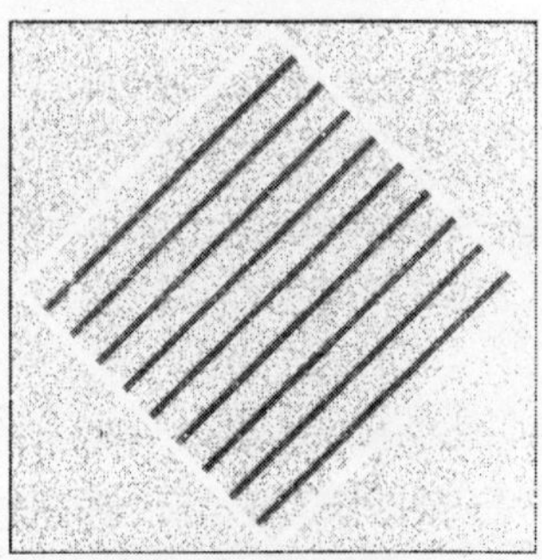

Rhombus

Activity

(i) *Material Required*: Sheet of paper.
(ii) *Description of the Activity*:

Teacher will try to make different geometrical figures like triangles, square, rectangle, parallelogram, rhombus etc. by folding paper. Students will be asked to define them. The teacher will then ask the students to make these figures by folding papers. With the help of this, properties of these shapes can be explained easily. Concept of perpendicular to a line and bisector of an angle can also be easily taught by paper folding activity.

9.2.5 Many Lines can be Drawn Through a Given Point

Rule: Many lines can be drawn through a given point

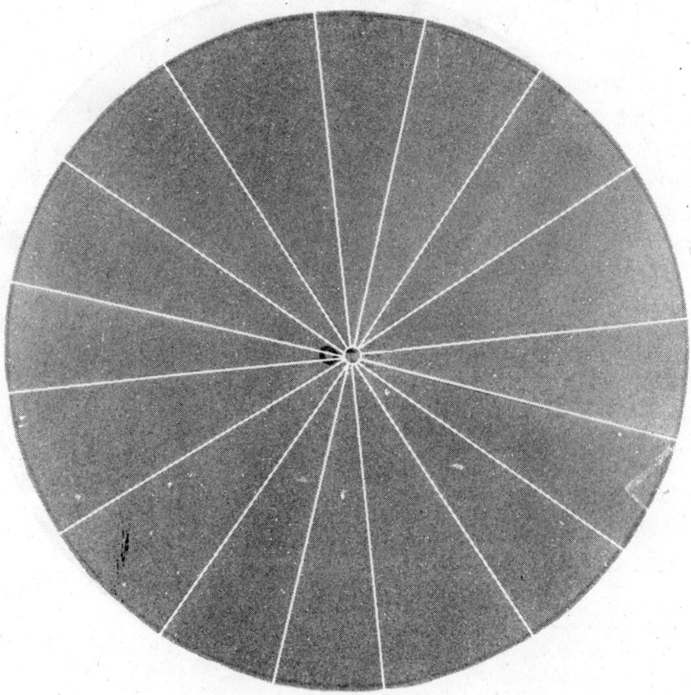

Activity

(i) *Material Required*: Sheet of paper.

(ii) *Description of the Activity*:

This concept can be easily given by the following activity:

Teacher will distribute a circle or a plain sheet of paper to each student. On each circle only one point is marked. The students will be asked to fold the sheet and make a crease in such a way that this crease will pass through that point. They can make as many crease as they want. Each creases represents one line. Now the students will be asked what they observed. Through this activity one can easily observe that, '*many lines can be drawn through a given point*'.

9.2.6 Only one Line can be Passed through Two Given Points

Rule: Only one line can be passed through two given points.

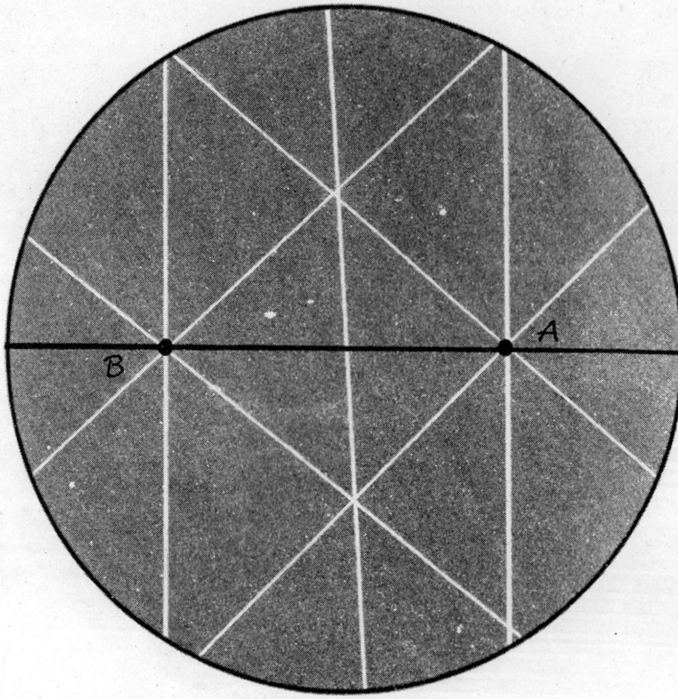

Activity

(i) *Material Required*: Sheet of paper.
(ii) *Description of the Activity*:

This concept can be easily given by the following activity:

Teacher will distribute a circle or a plane sheet of paper to each student. On each circle two points, say A and B are marked. The students are asked to fold the sheet and make a crease in such a way that this crease will pass through the two points. A and B. They can make as many crease as they want. Each crease will represent one line. Now the students will be asked what they observe. Through this activity one can easily observe that '*only one line can be drawn through two given points*'.

9.2.7. Among all the Line segments Drawn from a Given Point to a Given Line Perpendicular Line segment is the Shortest

Rule: Among all the line segments drawn from a given point to a given line, perpendicular line segment is the shortest.

Activity

(i) *Material Required*: Sheet of paper.

(ii) *Description of the Activity*:

To give the above-mentioned concept teacher can do the following activity:

- Draw a straight-line *t*. Take a point P outside *t*. From P fold the paper to draw perpendicular PQ to *t* intersecting it at Q. Now take point R on *t* and join P and R, by folding the paper.
- ΔPQR is a right angled triangle in which $\angle PQR$ is a right angle and PR is its hypotenuse.
- We know that in a right angled triangle, hypotenuse is the longest side.

Therefore, $PQ < PR$

This statement is true for every point other than Q lying on *t*.

So, we can say that—

Among all the line segments drawn from a given point to a given line, perpendicular line segment is the shortest. Or this concept can be given like this;

Draw a straight-line *t*. Take a point P outside *t*. From P fold the paper many times to get different lines from point P to line *t*. Now ask the students to find the shortest line from these lines. It may be easily concluded that *perpendicular line segment is the shortest one*.

9.2.8 Types of Angles

Rule: Different types of angles.

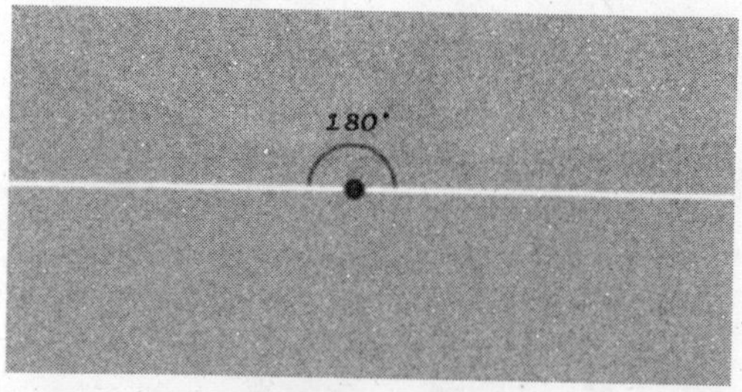

Straight Angle

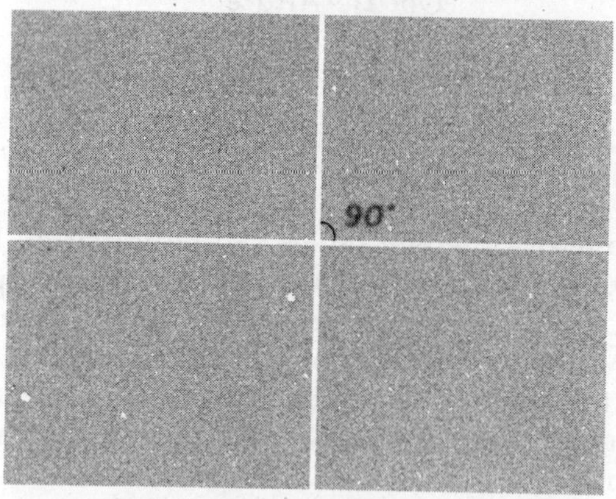

Right Angle

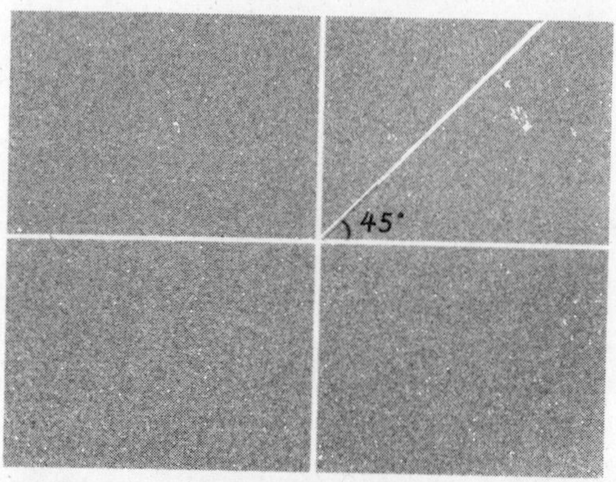

Acute Angle

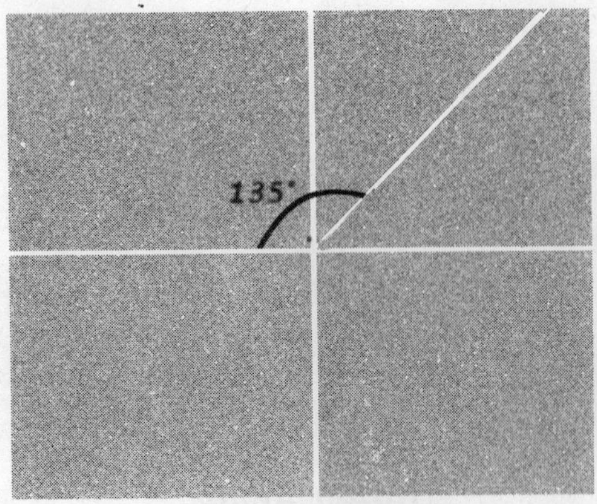

Obtuse Angle

Activity

(i) *Material Required*: Sheet of paper.

(ii) *Description of the Activity:*

Knowledge of different angles can be imparted by paper folding activities *e.g.* if we fold a paper in two equal parts and then open it, it will make the angle of 180°. If we again fold the paper into two then we get the angle of 90°. By folding one more time we get the angle of 45°. In the same way concept of acute and obtuse angles, complementary and supplementary angles can also be given.

9.2.9. Angle Sum Property of Triangle

Rule: Sum of three angles of a triangle is 180°.

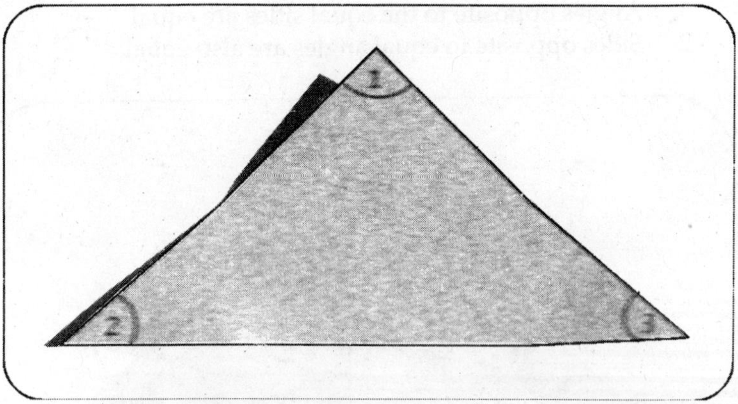

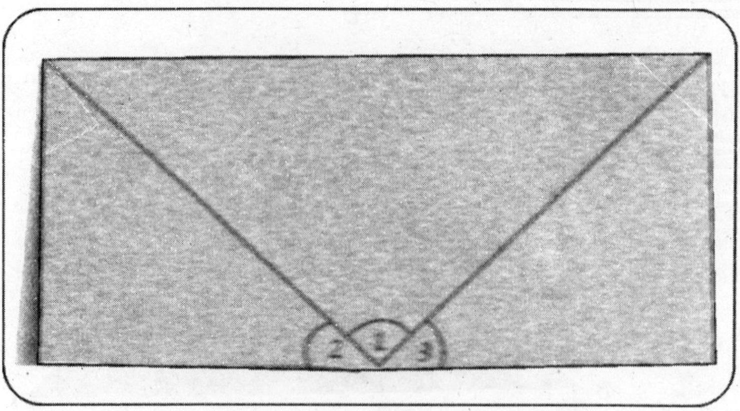

Activity

(i) *Material Required*: Sheet of paper.
(ii) *Description of the Activity:*

The concept of angle sum property of a triangle can be given by paper folding activity. For this, teacher will take a paper in a triangular shape and then ask the students to fold the three angles of the triangle as shown in the above figure.

By this activity, students can easily observe that these *three angles form a straight line, hence their sum will be 180°.*

9.2.10. Properties of Isosceles Triangles

Rule: In an isosceles triangle:

1. Angles opposite to the equal sides are equal.
2. Sides opposite to equal angles are also equal.

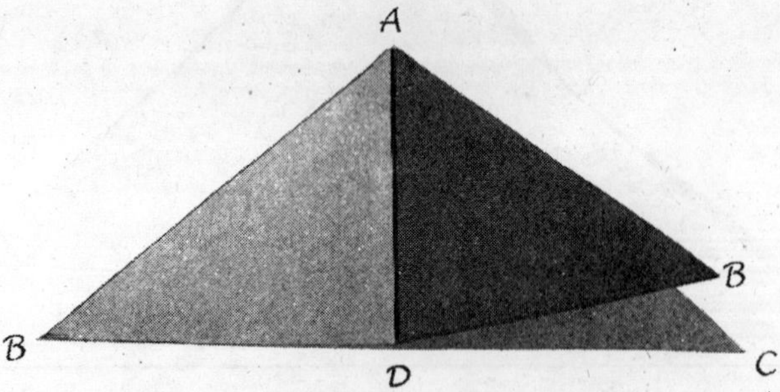

Two triangles for activity (isosceles triangle)

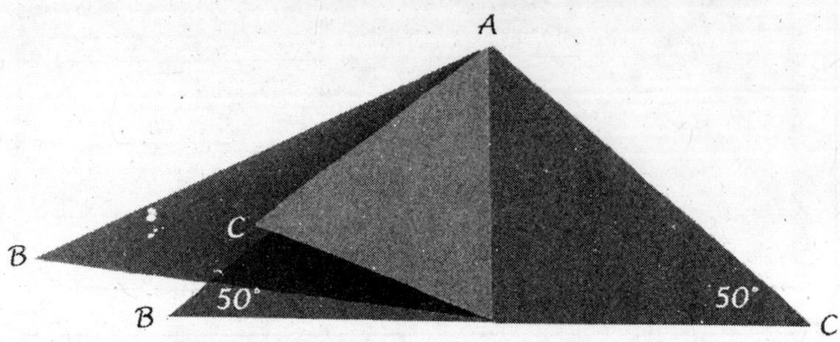

Two triangles for activity (isosceles triangle)

Activity

(i) *Material Required*: Triangle made of sheet of paper.
(ii) *Description of the Activity:*

With the help of following activity, properties of an isosceles triangle can be taught easily.

Construct a triangle ABC such that AB = AC = 35cm. Fold it so that AC falls along AB. Press to get a crease. Unfold the paper and draw line segment AD along the crease (as shown in the figure) meeting BC at D. Fold it again so that AB falls along AC and BD falls along CD.

Observe that ∠C covers ∠B exactly showing that ∠ABC = ∠ACD.

So, it can be concluded that in a triangle, *if two sides are equal, then the angles opposite to the equal sides are also equal.* This is the first property of an isosceles triangle.

Another activity can be done to give the concept of the second property.

Construct a triangle with ∠B = ∠C = 50°. Fold it so that ∠B falls on ∠C and the two parts of side BC cover each other exactly. Press to get a crease. It can be observed that the crease passes through A so that AC covers AB exactly. This shows that AC = AB.

Thus, it is concluded that:

In a triangle, *if two angles are equal, then the sides opposite to these angles are also equal.* This is the second property of an isosceles triangle.

9.2.11 Centroid of a Triangle

Rule: Medians intersect each other at the same point called centroid.

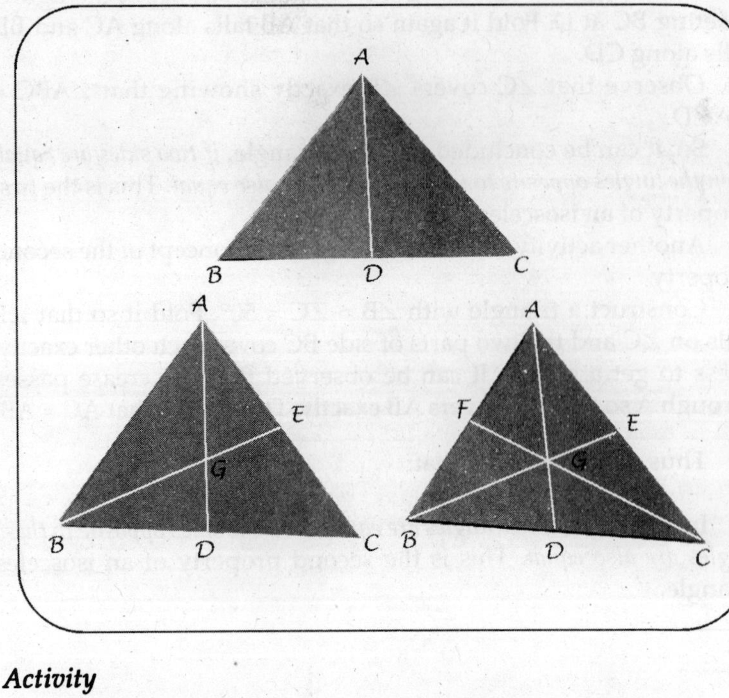

Activity

(i) *Material Required*: Triangle made by sheet of paper.
(ii) *Description of the Activity:*

It is a very difficult job to find centroid of a triangle. But, it can be easily understood by paper folding activity. For this, take a triangle made up of paper and fold its sides to get the mid-point of the sides and open it. Now fold the triangle in such a way that the mid-point of one side and the vertex opposite to this side comes in the same line and press it to make a crease. Repeat this activity for each side, as shown in the above photograph. With this activity we learn that:

'Three line segments (median) pass through the same point.

Or

Medians intersect each other at the same point and this point is known as centroid.'

9.2.12. Equal Chords of a Circle are Equidistant from the Centre

Rule: Equal chords of a circle are equidistant from the centre.

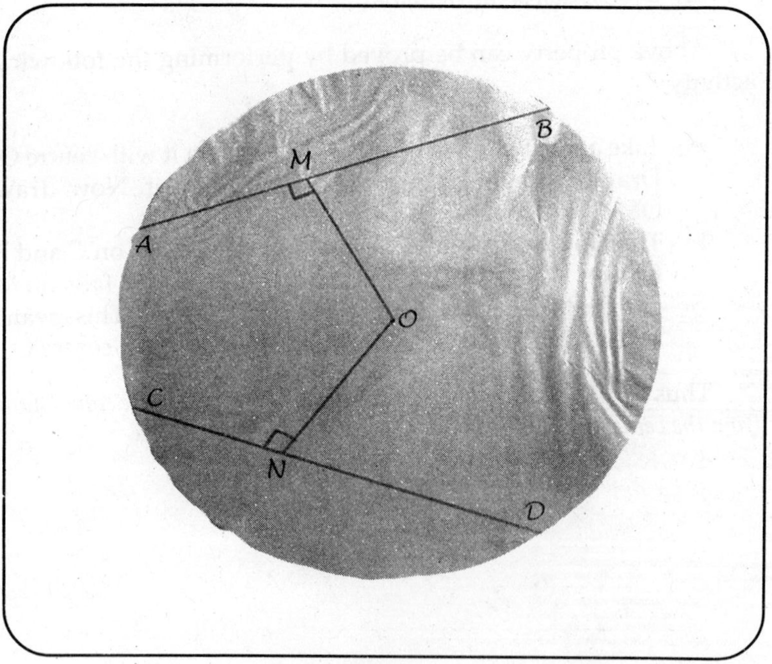

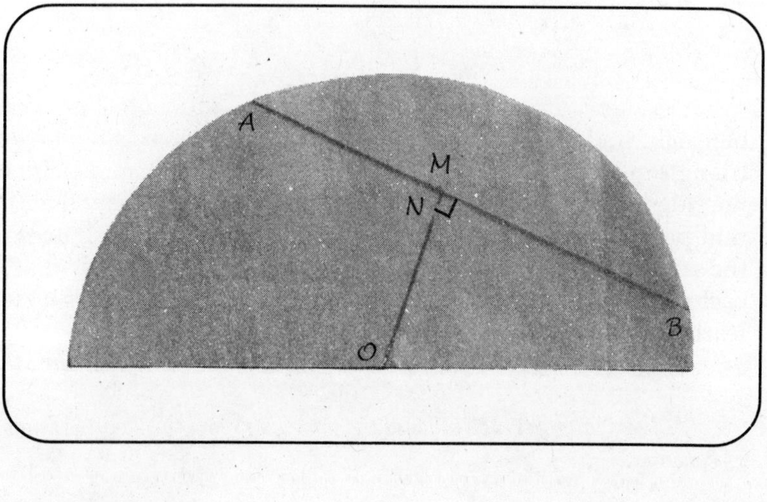

Activity

(i) *Material Required*: Sheet of paper.
(ii) *Description of the Activity.*

Above property can be proved by performing the following activity:

- Take a tracing paper and draw a circle on it with centre O. Draw two equal chords AB and CD on it. Now draw OM ⊥ AB and ON ⊥ CD.
- Then fold the paper, in such a way that A falls on C and B falls on D, as AB = CD then we observe that N falls on M and the line of fold passes through the center O. This means OM = ON *i.e.*, AB and CD are equidistant from centre O.

Thus we can conclude that: "*Equal chords of a circle are equidistant from the centre*".

9.2.13 Length of two Tangents, Drawn from a Given Point Outside the Circle are Equal

Rule: Length of two tangents drawn from a given point outside the circle are equal.

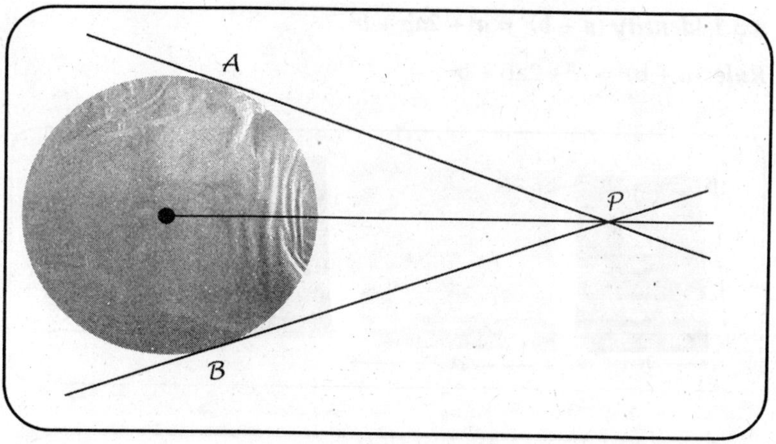

Activity

(i) *Material Required*: Circle made by a thick sheet of paper, tracing paper.

(ii) *Description of the Activity*:

This concept can be easily given by the following activity:

- The teacher will distribute to each student a circle made of thick sheet of paper pasted on a tracing paper, with a point (say) P marked outside the circle.
- The students will be asked to fold the sheet through the point P and make a crease in such a way that this crease will be the tangent to the circle.
- They can make as many creases as they want. Each crease will represent one tangent.
- Now the students will be asked as to how many tangents can they find through P and what did they observe about the length of these tangents?

Through this activity they can easily get the concept that *only two tangents can be drawn to a circle from a point outside it and the lengths of two tangents drawn from a given point outside the circle are equal.*

9.3 Paper Cutting and Pasting Activities

By cutting and pasting them, papers can also be used to clarify some difficult concepts. Students get permanent and long lasting knowledge of these concepts. Some activities are explained here.

9.3.1 *Identity* $(a + b)^2 = a^2 + 2ab + b^2$

Rule: $(a + b)^2 = a^2 + 2ab + b^2$

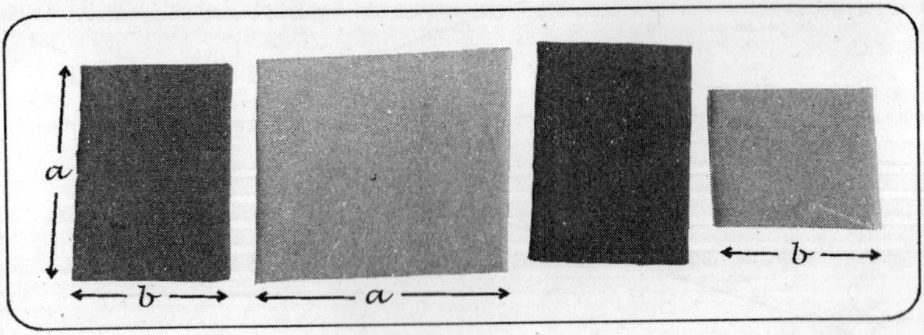

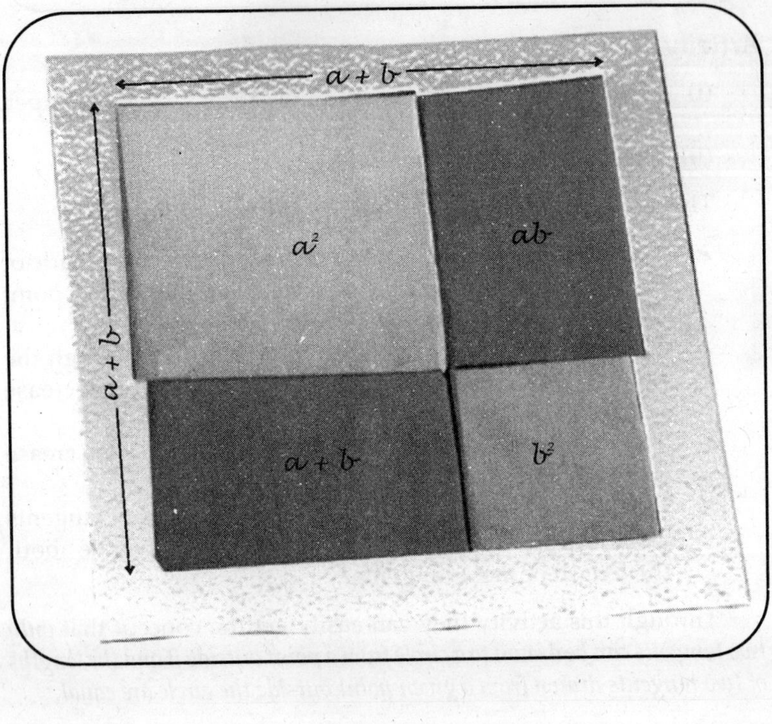

Activity

(i) *Material Required*: Sheet of paper.
(ii) *Description of the Activity:*

Two rectangles of measurement say 'a' unit and 'b' unit, and two squares of sides 'a' unit and 'b' unit respectively are shown to the students and they are asked about the area of the rectangle and square. Then students were asked to form a square from these given parts. Finally, the area of the formed square is calculated, and the identity obtained by adding the area of two rectangles and two squares as shown in the photograph. *i.e.*,

$$(a + b)^2 = a^2 + ab + b^2 + ab$$
$$(a + b)^2 = a^2 + b^2 + 2ab$$

9.3.2 *Identity $(a - b)^2 = a^2 - 2ab + b^2$*

***Rule*:** $(a - b)^2 = a^2 - 2ab + b^2$

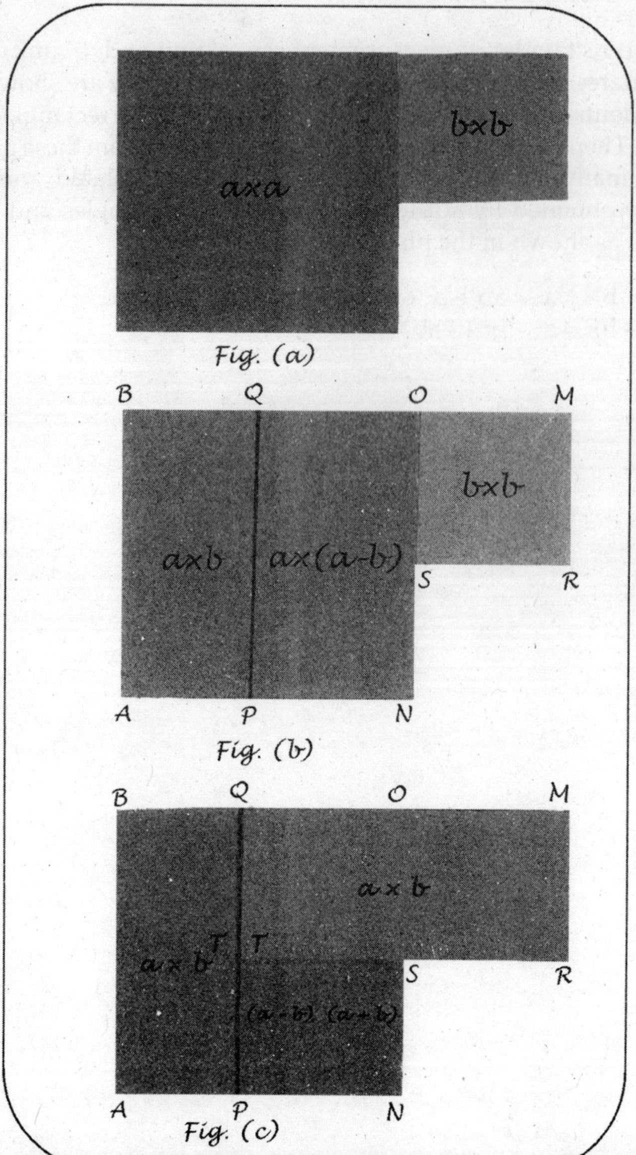

Activity

(i) *Material Required*: Sheet of paper.
(ii) *Description of the Activity:*

This identity can be easily taught by the following activity. For this take two squares of sides 'a' unit and 'b' unit as shown in the photograph. Now ask the students to draw a line PQ in the bigger square to divide it into two rectangles of dimensions a × b and a × (a – b) as shown in the photograph. Extend RS to complete the figure (c). We may regard the figure (c) as consisting of the rectangle APQB, rectangle RMQT and square PNST. Since

$$QM = (a - b) + b = a$$

And also $NS = NO - SO = AB - RM = a - b$, therefore,

$$\begin{aligned} a^2 + b^2 &= \text{area of fig. (a)} \\ &= \text{area of fig. (c)} \\ &= \text{area of rectangle APQB + area of rectangle RMQT + area of square PNST} \\ &= ab + ab + (a - b) \times (a - b) \end{aligned}$$

or $a^2 + b^2 = 2ab + (a - b)^2$ or

$$(a - b)^2 = a^2 - 2ab + b^2$$

9.3.3. Identity $(a + b)(a - b) = a^2 - b^2$

Rule: $(a + b)(a - b) = a^2 - b^2$

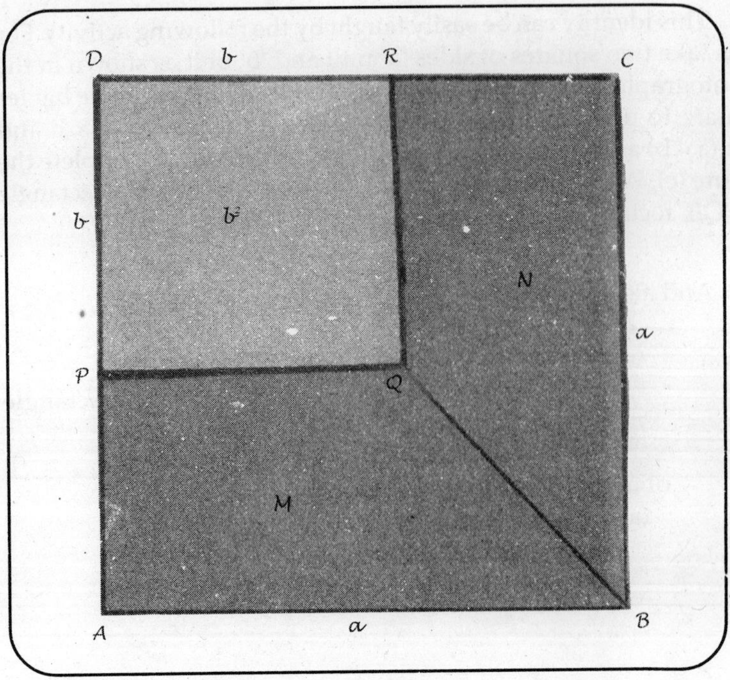

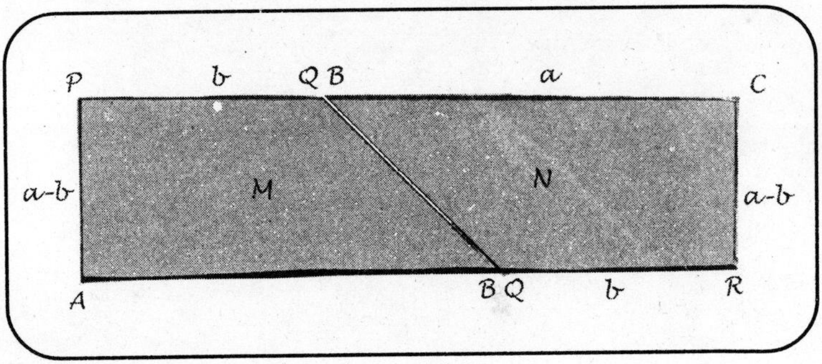

Activity

(i) *Material Required*: Sheet of paper.

(ii) *Description of the Activity:*

The above-mentioned identity is very difficult in itself, but with the help of paper cutting and pasting activity it can be demonstrated very easily. The activity is as follows:

- Take a square of length 'a'. So that its area is a^2. Cut a square of length b ($b < a$) from the square.
- Cut the rest of the figure into two equal parts as shown in the figure.
- Arrange them in such a way that they will form a geometrical figure.

The area of the obtained figure = $(a + b)(a - b)$
Thus, we get

$$a^2 - b^2 = (a + b)(a - b)$$

9.3.4 Identity $(x + a)(x + b) = x^2 + (a + b)x + ab$

Rule: $(x + a)(x + b) = x^2 + (a + b)\,x + ab$

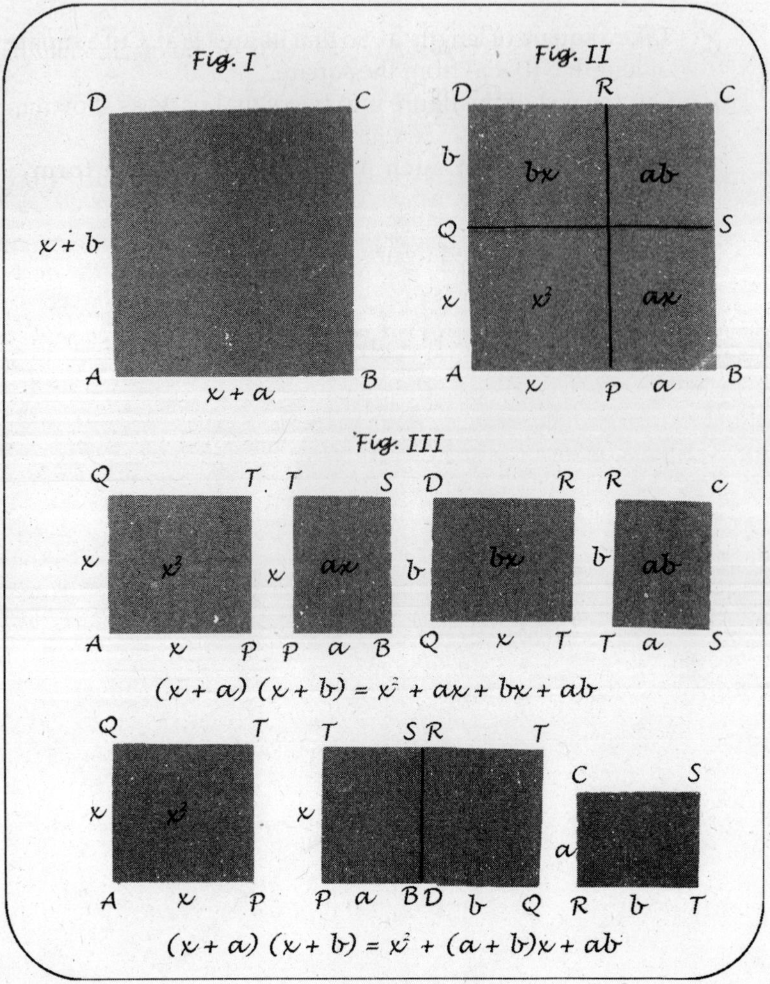

Activity

(i) *Material Required*: Sheet of paper.

(ii) *Description of the Activity:*

This activity is very complicated in itself but with the help of paper cutting and pasting activity it can be demonstrated very easily. The activity goes as follows:

- Take a piece of paper in rectangular shape of dimensions (say) x + a and x + b (e.g., ABCD of fig. I).
- Draw a line (say RP) to separate the length x + a as x and a, similarly draw a line x + b as x and b (fig. II).
- By doing this activity we get one square and three rectangles. Now arrange them as shown in fig. III.
- It can be observed easily that area of fig. I should be equal to the area of fig. III. Which is the required identity.

9.3.5. The Sum of Three Angles of a Triangle is 180°

Rule: The sum of three angles of a triangle is 180°.

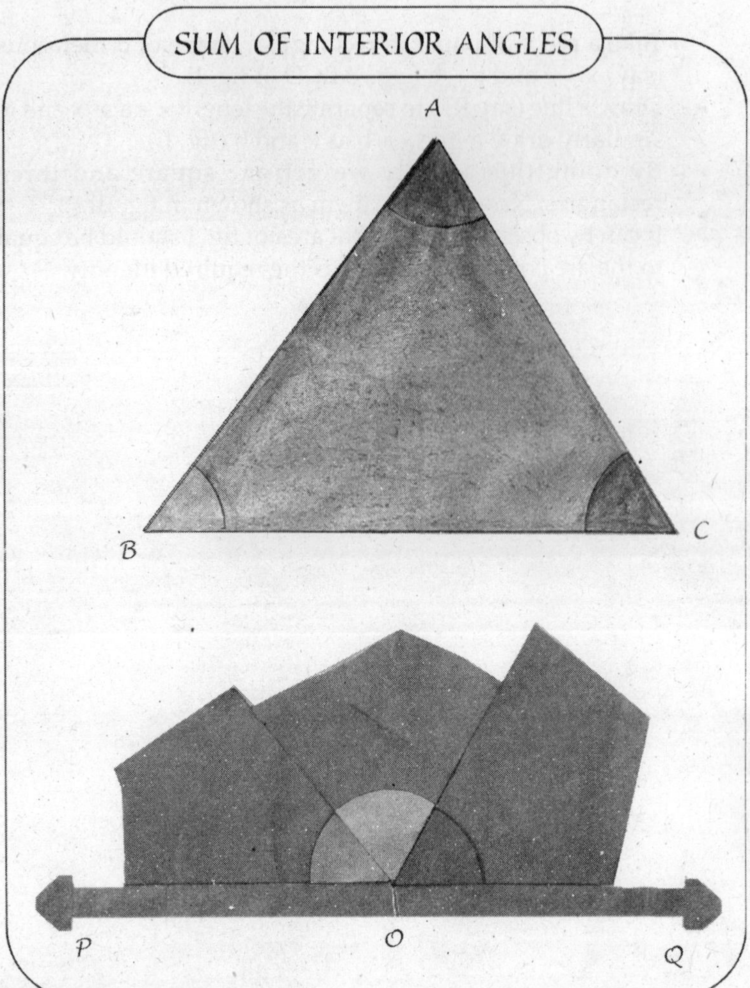

Activity

(i) *Material Required*: Thick sheet of paper

(ii) *Description of the Activity:*

The above-mentioned property can be explained by the following activity:

- A triangle made of thick sheet of paper labelled ABC with angles marked as $\angle 1$, $\angle 2$ and $\angle 3$ is displayed on the black board. Students are then told that since they are concerned with three angles of the triangles. So they should cut these angles and place them together and notice what happens.
- For doing this activity one student is asked to cut out angles numbered 1, 2 and 3 and another student is asked to place them at point O of the line PQ.
- Students will see for themselves that $\angle 1$, $\angle 2$ and $\angle 3$ make a straight line *i.e.* the sum of $\angle 1$, $\angle 2$ and $\angle 3$ is 180° or the sum of three angles of a triangle is 180°.

This activity can be done individually by giving paper made triangles to each student.

9.3.6 Exterior Angle of a Triangle is Equal to the Sum of the Two Interior Opposite Angles

Rule: If a side of a triangle is extended, the exterior angle of the triangle formed is equal to the sum of the two interior opposite angles.

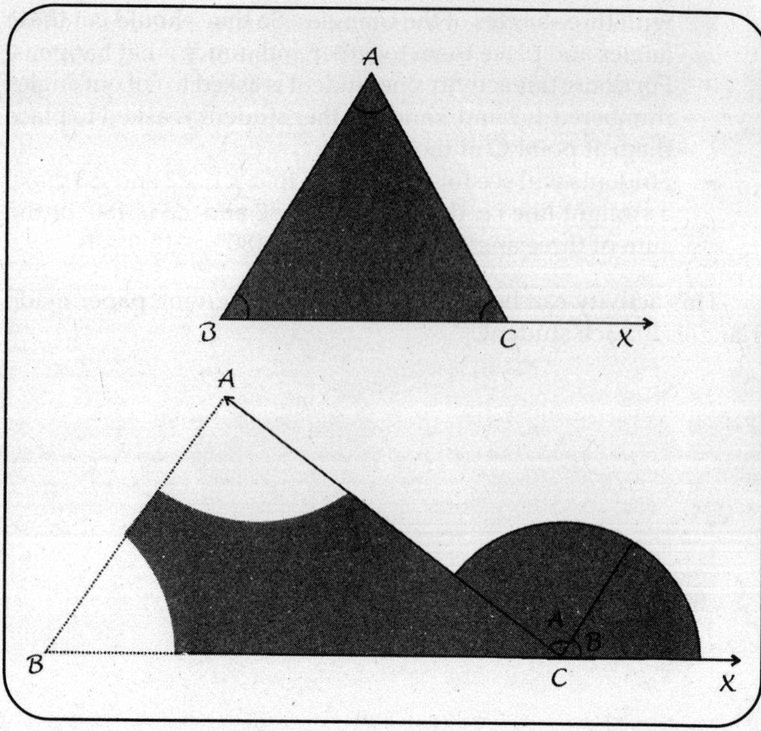

Activity

(i) *Material Required*: Thick sheet of paper.
(ii) *Description of the Activity*:

The above property can be easily proved practically with the help of the following activity:

- Each student of a class is provided with a triangle pasted over a sheet of paper such that ∠ACX represents exterior angle. A similar teaching aid is pasted over the board, also.

- Students are asked to trace the side AC of ∠ACB such that ∠ACX remains intact even if the triangle ABC is removed from the sheet. The students are then asked to cut the angles ∠BAC and ∠ABC. Since the concern is to see the measure of exterior angle ∠ACX. This is why, students are asked to place ∠BAC and ∠ABC over ∠ACX.
- Students will see for themselves that ∠BAC and ∠ABC have completely overlapped exterior angle *i.e.*, ∠ACX = ∠BAC + ∠ABC.

Thus, it can be concluded that—

$$\angle ACX = \angle BAC + \angle ABC$$

In other words, *Exterior angle is equal to the sum of two interiors opposite angles.*

9.3.7. The Sum of any Two Sides of a Triangle is Greater than the Third Side

Rule: Sum of two sides of a triangle is greater than the third side

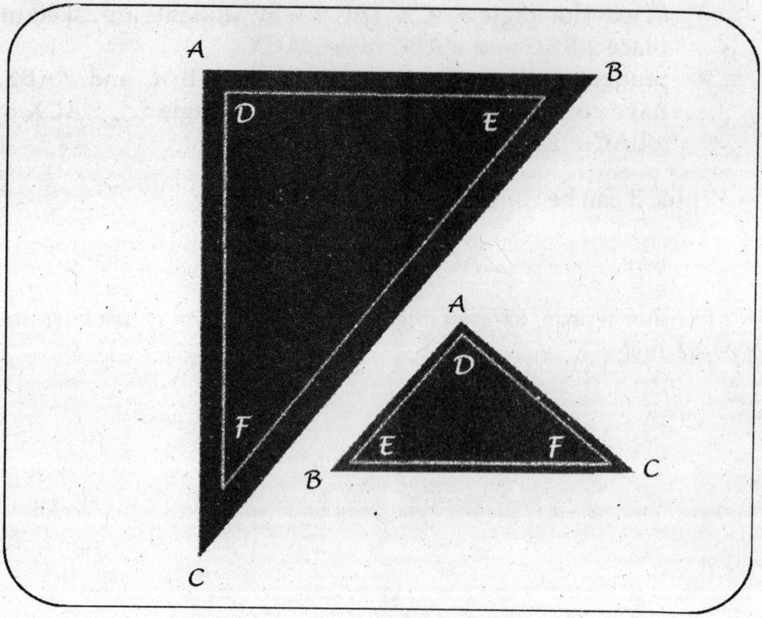

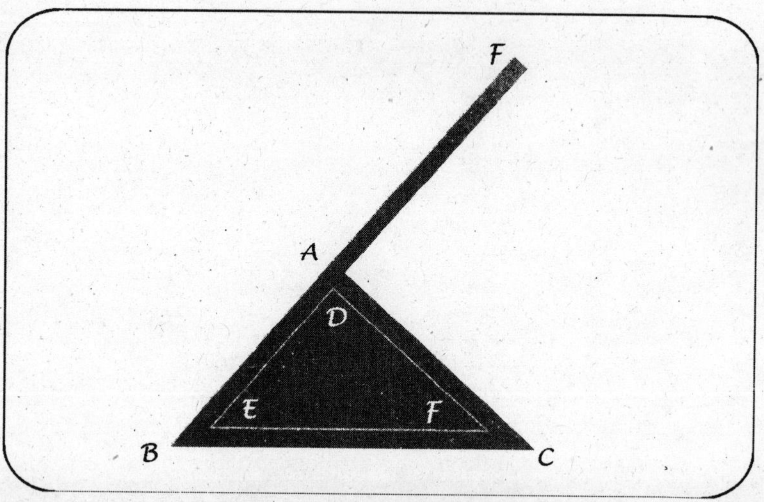

Activity

(i) *Material Required*: Thick sheet of paper
(ii) *Description of the Activity:*

To prove this property following activity can be done:

- Each student of the class is provided a big triangle made up of thick sheet of paper. Inside this triangle another smaller triangle DEF is taken (rather marked).
- Students are asked to cut side DF and place it in such a way that EDF forms a straight line.
- Then student are asked to measure the line EDF and line EF.
- On comparing both types the students will find that length of side EDF is greater than EF' *i.e.*, ED + DF > EF

In other words they can easily observe that, *Sum of any two sides of a triangle is greater than the third side.*

9. 3.8 The Mid-Point Theorem

Rule: A line drawn through the mid-points of the two sides of a triangle is parallel to the third side and its length is half of the third side.

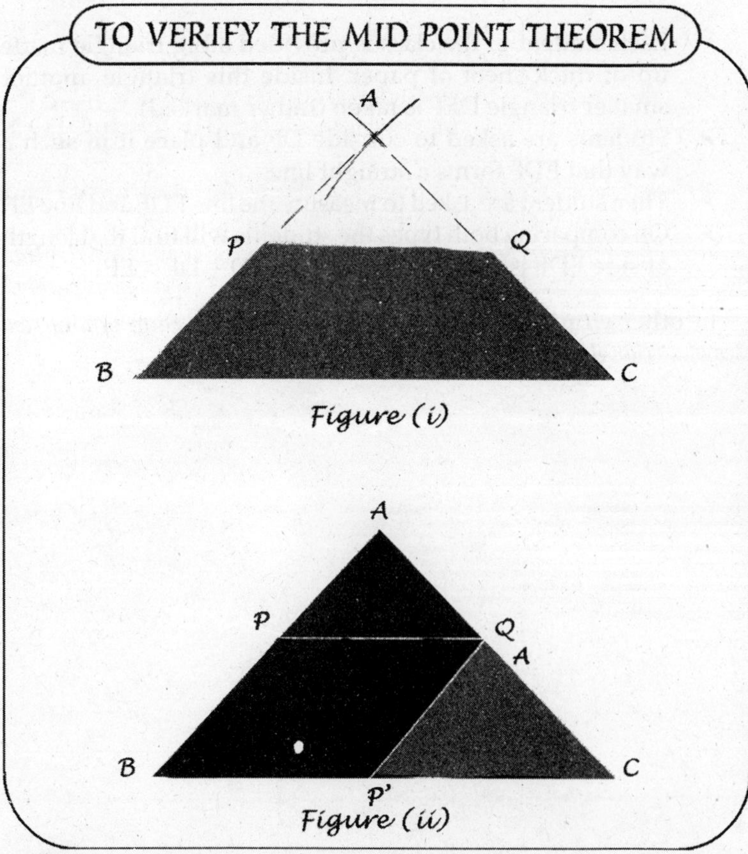

Activity

(i) *Material Required*: Thick sheet of paper.

(ii) *Description of the Activity:*

To prove this property practically the following activity will be helpful:

- Triangle made up by a thick sheet of paper (say ABC) will be distributed to each student.
- The students will be asked to mark the mid-points (say P and Q) of any two sides of the triangle (say AB and AC respectively) and join them and then cut the small triangle ΔAPQ and place it on ΔABC as shown in photograph.
- Then students are asked to measure ∠AP′C and ∠P′QP and line P′C and P′B.
- On comparing these angles students will find that ∠APC = P′QP, but these are alternate angles therefore line PQ is parallel to line BC.
- On comparing these lines *i.e.*, P′C and P′B, students find that P′C = P′B *i.e.*, P is the mid-point of line BC.
- From this activity students can easily observe that, '*A line drawn through the mid-points of two sides of a triangle is parallel to the third side and its length is half of the third side*'.

9.3.9 The Ratio of the Lengths of Median is 2:1

Rule: The ratio of the lengths of median is 2:1.

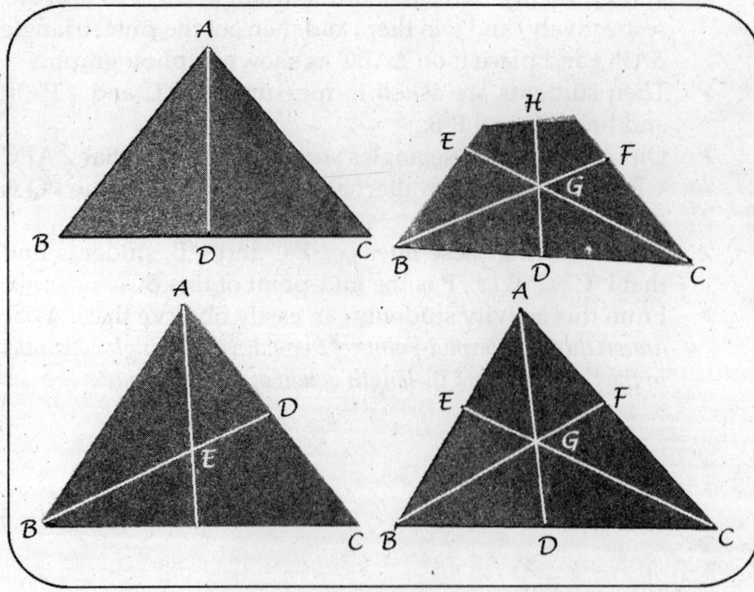

Activity

(i) *Material Required*: Sheet of paper.

(ii) *Description of the Activity:*

Although this is a very difficult concept, but it can be easily taught with the help of following activity.

Find the centroid of a triangle by paper folding activity as discussed in 9.2.5. After that fold any one of the vertices to meet the centroid and cut it. Put the cut part on rest of the median (below centroid). Now measure the length from vertex to centroid *i.e.*, GD and centroid to the side of the triangle *i.e.*, GH and HA; it will be find that all these three are equal *i.e., the ratio of the lengths of median i.e., AG : GD is 2:1* which is required proparty.

9.3.10 Angle Sum Property of Quadrilateral

Rule: Sum of four angles of a quadrilateral is 360°.

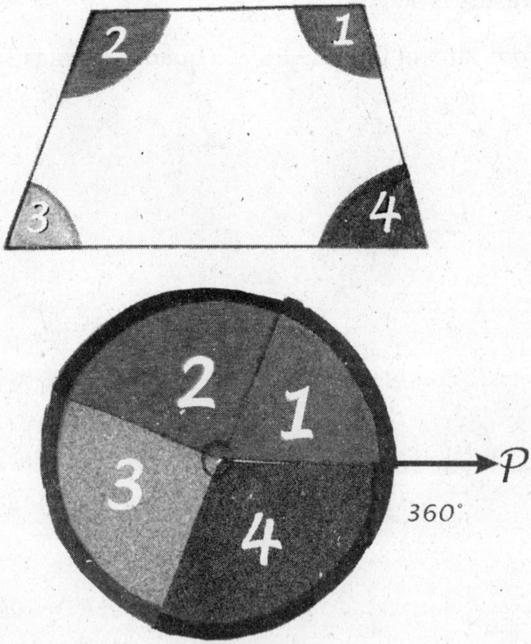

Activity

(i) *Material Required*: Thick sheet of paper.
(ii) *Description of the Activity:*

To practically prove this property,

- Take a thick sheet of paper and draw a quadrilateral ABCD. Mark the four angles as ∠1, ∠2, ∠3, and ∠4.
- Cut out the quadrilateral ABCD along its sides with a pair of scissors. Now cut the four arcs showing four angles of a quadrilateral.
- Draw a ray OP on a sheet of paper. Arrange four cut out angles (without overlapping) in such a way that vertex of each angle falls on O.

➢ Start with $\angle 1$ putting one of its arms along ray OP. Place the other angles one by one so that no two of them overlap and no gaps are left. Students will find that four angles formed at O together make up the complete angle whose measure is 360°.

Therefore, sum of four angles of a quadrilateral is 360°

9.3.11 Properties of a Parallelogram

Rule: The four properties of a parallelogram are as follows:

1. A diagonal of a parallelogram divides it into two congruent triangles.
2. Opposite sides of a parallelogram are equal.
3. Opposite angles of a parallelogram are equal.
4. Diagonals of a parallelogram bisect each other.

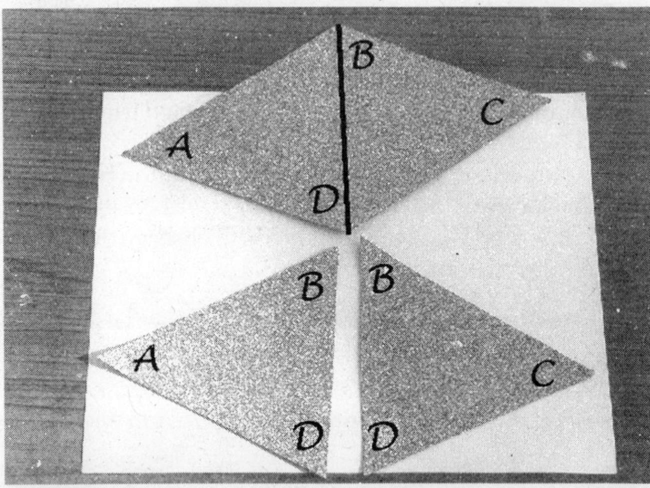

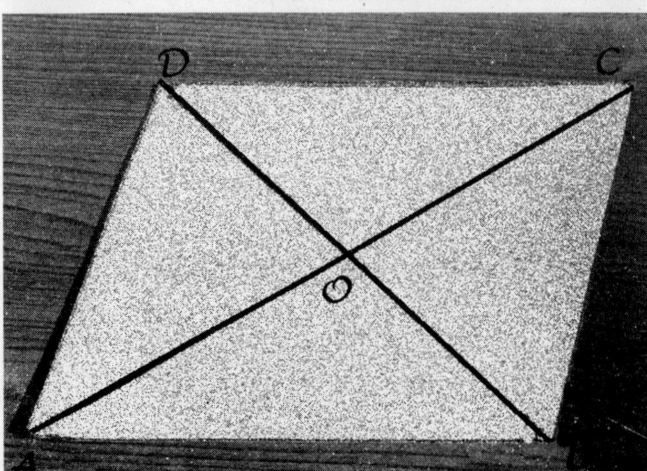

Activity

(i) *Material Required*: Chart paper, sheet of paper.
(ii) *Description of the Activity:*

Properties of a parallelogram can be demonstrated with the help of this activity:

- A parallelogram made up of thick sheet of paper with diagonal BD joined is distributed to the whole class.
- The students are asked to concentrate on the diagonal BD of parallelogram ABCD and are asked to fold the parallelogram along the line BD. They are then asked to cut it into two halves, so that they get two triangles, ΔABD and ΔCBD.
- The students are asked to establish a relation between these two triangles.
- By superimposing, the students will observe that, these two triangles are congruent.

Thus, the first property of parallelogram is established. According to this—

'The diagonal of a parallelogram divides it into two congruent triangles.'

Since these two triangles are congruent so, the other properties of parallelogram can be automatically inferred from corresponding parts of congruenτ parts *i.e.* c.p.c.t.

By c.p.c.t.

$$AB = CD \text{ and } BC = AD \text{ (since } \Delta ABC \cong \Delta CDA)$$

'In a parallelogram, the opposite sides are equal'
Similarly, By c.p.c.t.

$\angle B = \angle D$ (if we consider AC as diagonal)
and $\angle A = \angle C$ (if we consider BD as diagonal)

Thus, third property says:

'In a parallelogram, the opposite angles are equal'

In the end, students are asked to join both the diagonals of parallelogram ABCD and infer from ΔAOB & ΔCOD if O is the point of intersection of diagonals AC and BD.

The observations are as follows:

Since $AB = CD$

$\angle OBA = \angle ODC$

$\angle OAB = \angle OCD$

Therefore, $\Delta AOB \cong \Delta COD$ (ASA)

By c.p.c.t $AO = CO, BO = OD$

Thus, students have learnt the fourth property of a parallelogram

'In a parallelogram, the diagonals bisect each other'

9.3.12 Parallelogram on the Same Base and between Same Parallel Lines are Equal in Area

Rule: Parallelogram on the same base and between same parallel lines are equal in area.

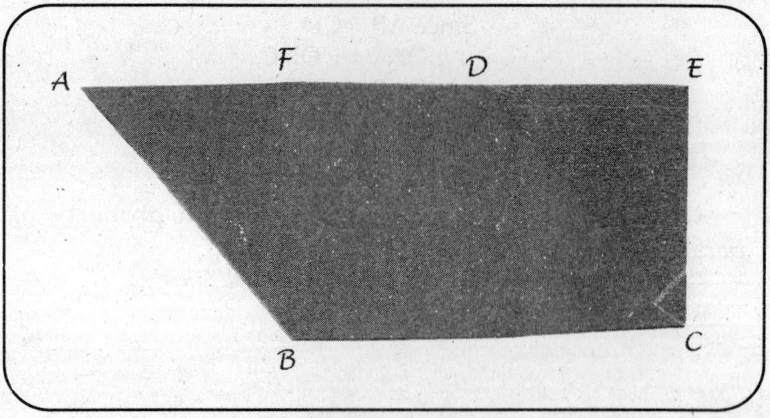

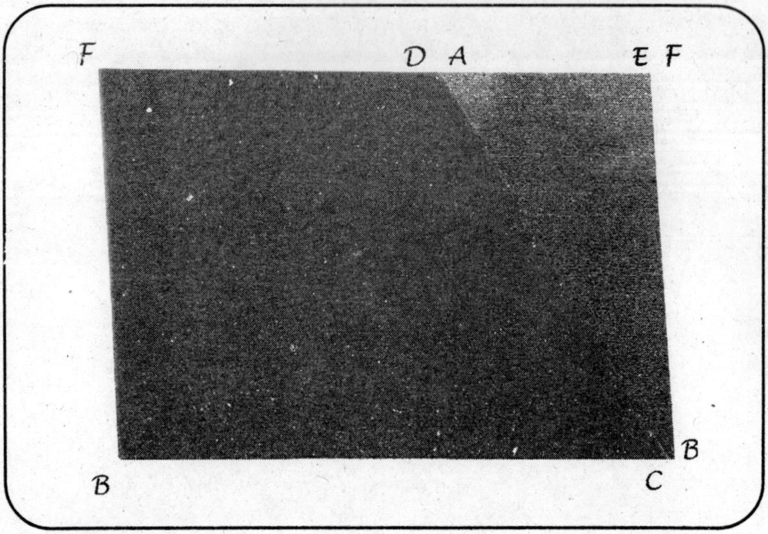

Activity

(i) *Material Required*: Chart paper, sheet of paper.

(ii) *Description of the Activity:*

To prove this property, following activity can be done:

- Students of the class are given two parallelograms arranged on the same base and between the same parallel lines.
- These two parallelograms were named as ABCD and ECBF with common base BC.
- The students are then asked about the parallelogram ECBF which is nothing but a rectangle. They were familiar that the rectangle is a parallelogram.
- Students know that the area of rectangle ECBF = FB × BC.
- They are asked to find out the area of the parallelogram ABCD and are instructed to cut ΔAFB and place it over a ΔDEC. Students will realize that the area occupied by ABCD is same as that occupied by other parallelogram ECBF because ΔAFB has exactly overlapped the ΔDEC.

Hence, it can be conclude that;

'Parallelogram on the same base and between same parallel lines is equal in area.'

9.3.13 Area of a Parallelogram

Rule: The area of the parallelogram = Base × Height

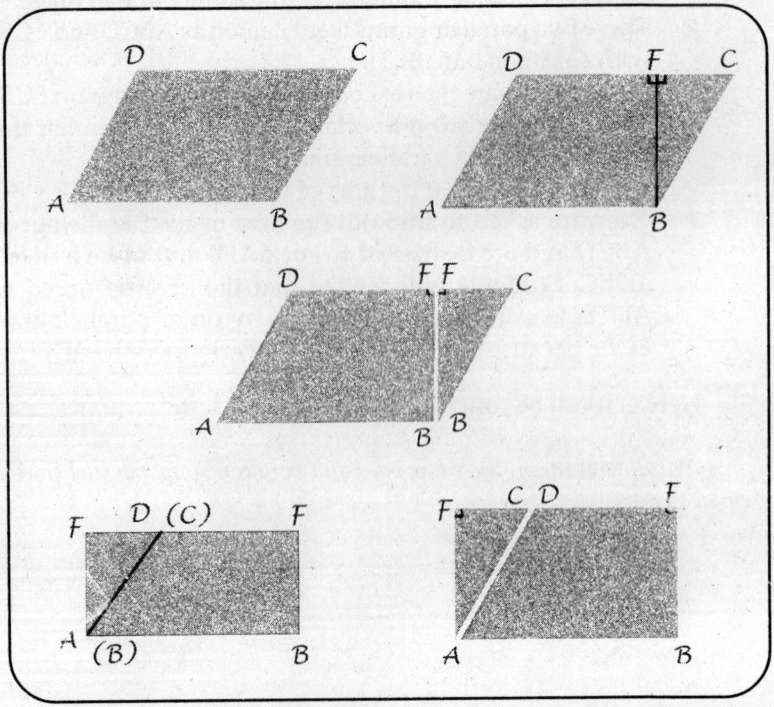

Activity

(i) *Material Required*: Sheet of paper.

(ii) *Description of the Activity:*

The following activity can be used to give the concept of area of a parallelogram:

- First, student were asked to draw a parallelogram ABCD. Now consider AB as the base, and draw an altitude BF *i.e.* BF ⊥ DC in such a way that both the angles DFB and BFC are right angles.
- Separate the ΔBCF by cutting along FB. Pick up the triangular piece ΔBCF and place it to the left of the other

piece ABFD. By sliding the triangular piece towards the other piece till BC coincides with AD.

- Student were observed that a new geometrical shape is obtained from the parallelogram by cutting and pasting without overlaps or gaps which is nothing but a rectangle with sides AB and BF. Hence, the area of the two pieces should equal.
- Thus, students can easily find out that—

Area of the rectangle = length × breadth
= AB × BF
= Base of the parallelogram ABCD × height

Hence, the area of the parallelogram
= AB × BF
= Base × Height

(As AB is the base of the given parallelogram and BF is its altitude or height.)

9.3.14 *Area of Trapezium*

Rule: Area of trapezium = 1/2 (sum of the parallel sides) × height

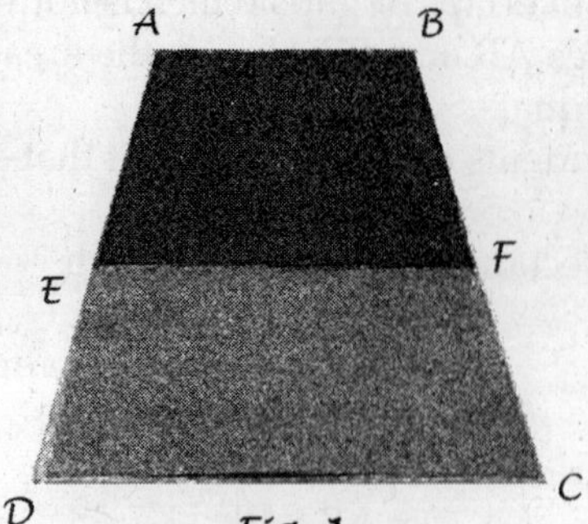

Fig. 1

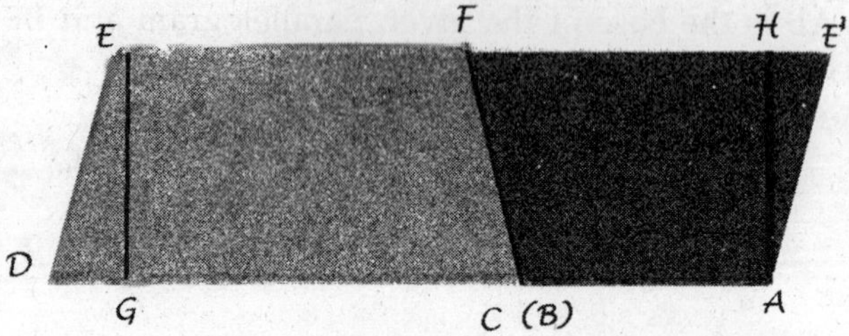

Fig. 2

Activity

(i) *Material Required*: Sheet of paper.
(ii) *Description of the Activity:*

Area of Trapezium can be taught with the help of following activity. Students are aware that, a trapezium is a quadrilaterals in which at least one pair of opposite sides is parallel. A quadrilateral ABCD is shown to the students, they can find that it is a trapezium because AB || DC and AB & CD are the bases of trapezium.

To find out the area of trapezium following activity can be done:

- Students were asked to draw a trapezium (say) ABCD.
- Teacher will ask students to draw a horizontal line between

the two bases of trapezium such that this line is parallel to both the bases and lies exactly in the centre (*i.e.* it passes through the mid-points of altitudes). This is shown in figure 1. Line EF is parallel to both AB and CD, and EF lies exactly in between AB and CD *i.e.* AE = ED and BF = FC. This line EF divides the trapezium into two parts or two quadrilaterals ABFE and EFCD. Students can see these two quadrilaterals distinctly.

- Now students are asked to cut the trapezium along EF and place the quadrilaterals in such a way that they together make a parallelogram. This is shown in figure 2.
- This way the students can deduce the area of a trapezium from the given area of parallelogram ADEE′

Area of parallelogram = base × height.
Base of parallelogram ADEE′ =AB + CD = AD
Height of parallelogram ADEE′ = AH = EG
Therefore the area of parallelogram ADEE′ = AD × AH

- Students can easily observe that:
  - *The area of trapezium ABCD =Area of parallelogram ADEE′* (because parallelogram was made from trapezium itself) = AD × AH.
  - Students can see that AD = AB + CD *i.e.* sum of parallelogram sides of the trapezium, and
  - AH =1/2 (the height of trapezium), because AE = ED and BF = FC. (Fig. 1).
- Therefore area of trapezium will be = (AB + CD) × ½ (the height of the trapezium).

Area of trapezium = 1/2 (sum of parallelogram sides) × height

9.3.15 Angles in the Same Segment

Rule: Angles in the same segment are equal.

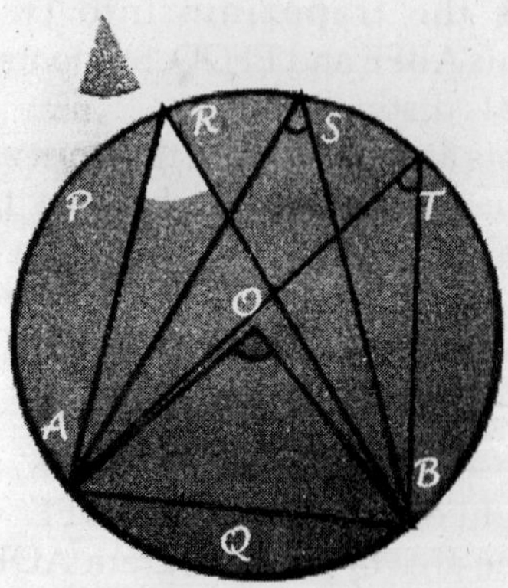

Fig. 1

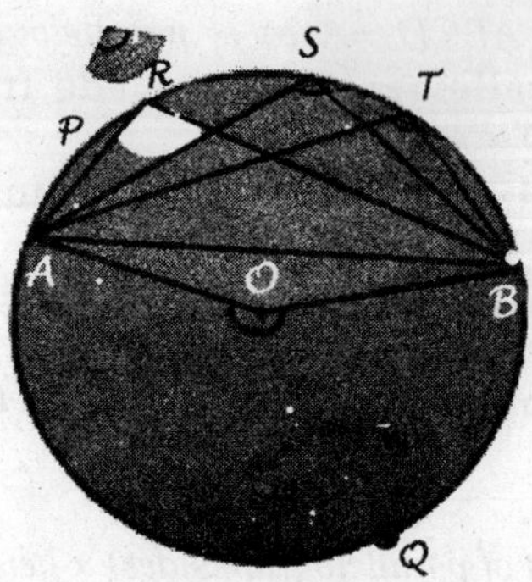

Fig. 2

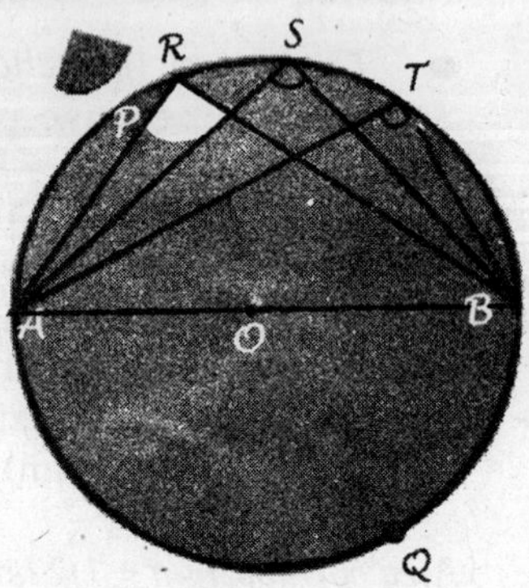

Fig. 3

Activity

(i) *Material Required*: Cardboard or chart, sheet of paper.

(ii) *Description of the Activity:*

This property can be depicted by the following activity:

In a circle with center O, a chord AB divides it into two segments APB and AQB.

Either of these two segments may be minor, major or equal. In fig. 1. APB is major segement and AQB is minor. In fig. 2. APB is minor segment and AQB is major segment. But in fig. 3. chord AOB is a diameter also, therefore both the segments APB and AQB are equal. In segments APB, there are three angles ∠ARB, ∠ASB and ∠ATB. Cut one of its angles and place it over the other angles. It will be observed that ∠ ARB covers ∠ASB and ∠ATB. Therefore we can say that ∠ARB = ∠ASB = ∠ATB. Logically also, this property can be established easily. Arc AQB subtends ∠AOB at the centre and the same arc inscribes ∠ARB, ∠ASB and ∠ATB on the remaining part of the circles. Therefore, each of these is half of ∠AOB. Therefore ∠ARB = ∠ASB = ∠ATB.

From this activity we may conclude that '*Angles in the same segment are equal*'.

9.3.16 A Cyclic Quadrilateral and Its Angles

Rule: Opposite angles of a cyclic quadrilateral are supplementary.

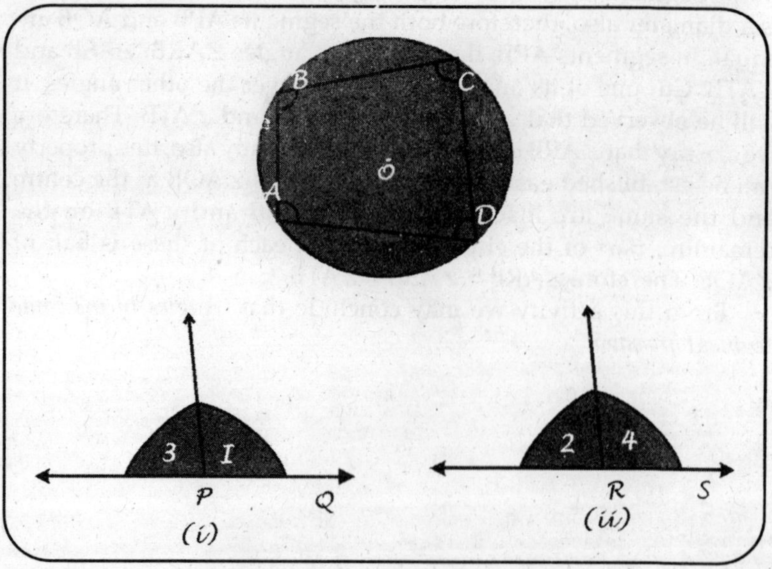

Fig. 1

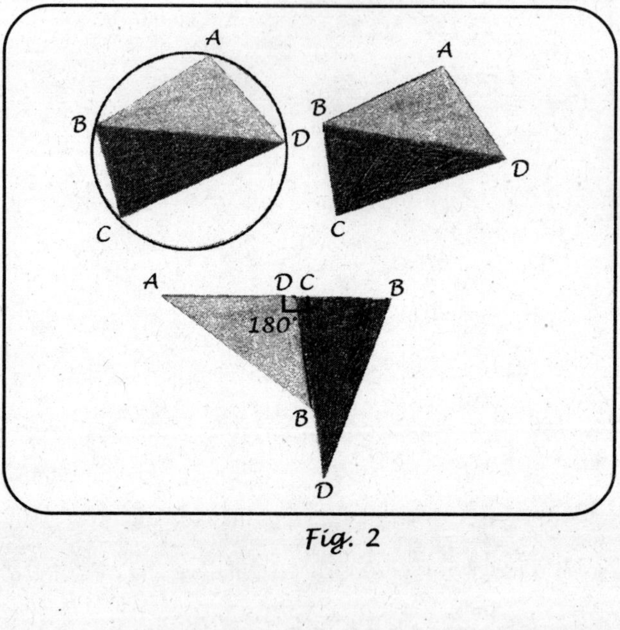

Fig. 2

Activitys

(i) *Material Required*: Sheet of paper.
(ii) *Description of the Activity:*

Two very good activities can be performed to get a practical understanding of the above said concept:

Draw a circle with center O and inscribe a quadrilateral ABCD in it. Label the four angles A, B, C and D as angles 1, 2, 3 and 4 respectively. Now draw a line PQ and place $\angle 1$ and $\angle 3$ with vertex of each angle lying at P and one arm of $\angle 1$ lying along ray PQ and the other arm coinciding with one arm of $\angle 3$ without any overlapping (fig. 1).

It will be seen that, $\angle 1 + \angle 3 = 180°$ *i.e.*, $\angle A + \angle C = 180°$
Similarly, by taking $\angle 2$ and $\angle 4$, it can be seen that,

$$\angle 2 + \angle 4 = 180° \text{ i.e., } \angle B + \angle D = 180°$$

Thus, the above activity shows that, '*Opposite angles of a cyclic quadrilateral are supplementary*'.

For the other activity, draw a circle and inscribe a quadrilateral ABCD in it. Draw a diagonal (say BD) which divide it into two triangles ΔABD and ΔCBD. Now separate these two triangles by cutting it and place them, as shown in fig. 2. Students can easily observe that $\angle C$ and $\angle D$ makes a linear pair i.e., their sum is 180°.

Thus, '*opposite angles of a cyclic quadrilateral are supplementary*'.

9.3.17 Angle made at the Centre of a Circle by Equal Arc or Chords

Rule: Two equal chords or two equal arcs subtend equal angles at the center of the circle.

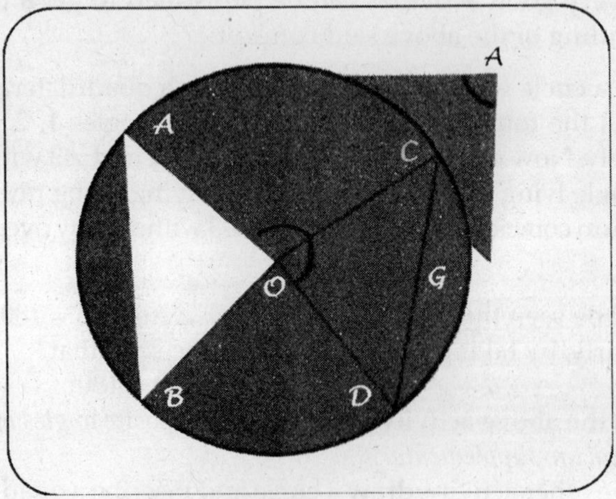

Activity

(i) *Material Required*: Sheet of paper.
(ii) *Description of the Activity:*

Following activity can be done to give this concept:

- Draw a circle of any radius taking O as centre. Construct two chords AB and CD in it. Join both ends A and B of AB to O and both ends C and D of CD also to O. Now AOB and COD are the two triangles.
- Cut out ΔAOB from the circle. Now try to keep the ΔAOB on ΔCOD in such a way that A falls on C and B falls on D. Observe whether O of ∠AOB covers O of ∠COD. If it is true then we can say that ∠AOB = ∠COD.

Therefore degree measure of AB = degree measure of CD.
Or degree measures of ∠AOB = degree measure of ∠COD.
So it can be concluded that,

Two equal chords or two equal arcs subtend equal angles at the centre of the circle.

9.3.18 Relation between Central Angle and Inscribed Angle

Rule: The angle subtended by an arc at the centre is twice the angle subtended by same arc at any point on the remaining arc of the circle.

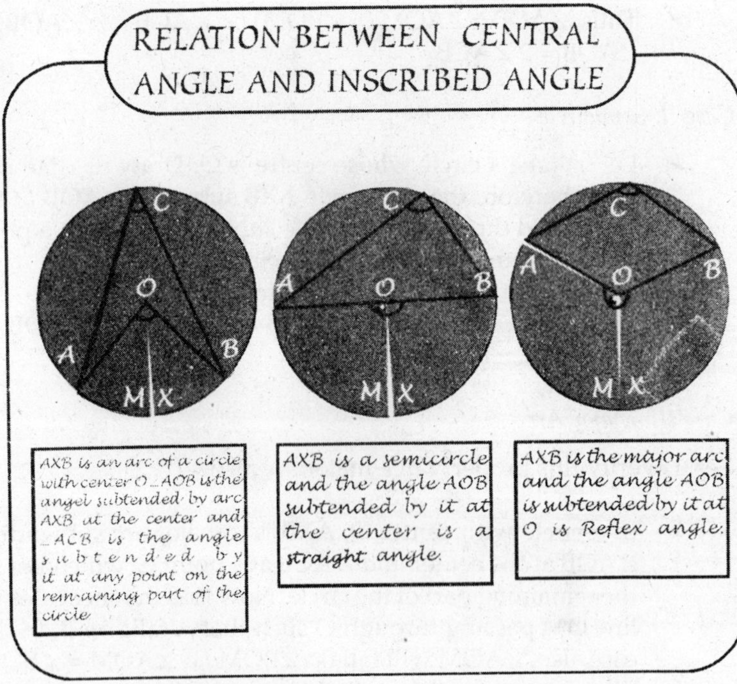

Activity

(i) *Material Required*: Sheet of paper.

(ii) *Description of the Activity:*

This relationship constitutes three cases:

Case I: Minor Arc

➢ Draw a circle with centre O. Take an arc AXB and mark a point C on the remaining part of the circle. Join AC and BC to obtain $\angle ACB$ and join OA and OB to obtain $\angle AOB$.

Now fold the sheet along a line OM passing through O, such that A falls on B. In this case, ∠AOM will fall on ∠BOM *i.e.* ∠AOM = ∠BOM. This means ∠AOM = ∠BOM = ½ ∠AOB.

- Now cut ∠AOM and place it over ∠ACB. You will observe that ∠AOM covers ∠ACB.
- Thus, ∠ACB = ∠AOM (= ∠BOM) *i.e.* ∠ACB = ½ ∠AOB, or ∠AOB = 2 ∠ACB.

Case II: Semicircle

- Let us take a circle whose centre is O. Draw its diameter AB. Therefore the semicircle AXB subtends ∠AOB at the centre and the same semicircle subtends ∠ACB at a point C on the remaining part of the circle.
- Now repeat the process on a semicircle.
- Here also ∠AOM covers ∠ACB *i.e.* ∠ACB = ½ ∠AOB, or ∠AOB = 2 ∠ACB

Case III: Major Arc

Let us verify this property in a major arc also.

- In a circle with center O, AXB is a major arc subtending ∠AOB at the center and ∠ACB at a point C, which lies on the remaining part of the circle. Now fold the sheet along a line OM passing through O such that A falls on B. In this case also, ∠AOM will fall on ∠BOM *i.e.* ∠AOM = ∠BOM. This means ∠AOM = ∠BOM = ½ ∠AOB
- Now cut ∠AOM and place it over ∠ACB and you will find that ∠AOM covers ∠ACB.
  Thus, ∠ACB = ½ ∠AOB or ∠AOB = 2 ∠ACB.

From these activities, we arrive to the conclusion that:

In a circle, *the angle subtended by an arc at the centre is twice the angle subtended by same arc at any point on the remaining arc of the circle.*

9.3.19 Area of Circle

Rule: Area of the circle = πr^2.

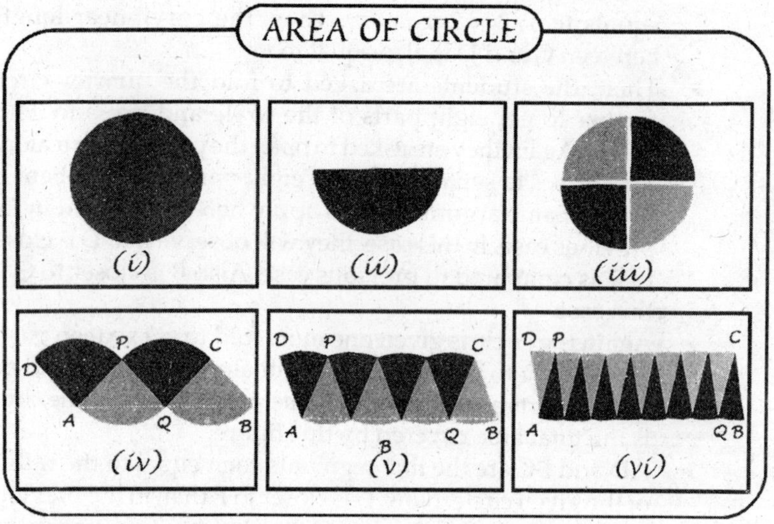

Activity

(i) *Material Required*: Sheet of paper.
(ii) *Description of the Activity:*

The following activity is an interesting and easy way to give the concept of area of a circle:

- Students are asked to draw a circle with radius '*r*', and fold one half of this circle over itself, in such a way that each part coincides with the other. Pressing along its diameter to get a crease. They are asked to fold the half circle again to get a quarter circle and press it along the bounding radii to get creases. They are then asked to open thr circle and cut along the creases to separate out four quarters and place them in such a way that the vertex of one piece is in the upward direction and the vertex of another piece is in the downward direction so on. The figure obtained by doing this activity clearly shows that, the area of the circle is equivalent to the total area covered by this figure.

- Students through this activity will observe that the line segments AD and BC each are equal to the radius of the given circle. Also, the length of the curvilinear part between A and B is equal to half of the circumference and therefore equals to $1/2 \times 2\pi r$ *i.e.* πr. Thus, the curvilinear length between C and D is also equal to πr.
- Then, the students are asked to fold the quarter circle further to get eight parts of the circle and press to get a crease. Again they are asked to open the circle and cut along the creases to separate out the eight parts placing them as before. Same arguments will apply here as they did in the previous case. In this case, they will observe that D is closer to P as compared to previous case. Also B is closer to Q in this case.
- Again the circle is given one more fold to get sixteen parts. Press along to get a crease and cut along the creases to get sixteen parts and place them as before. The area of the circle is the total area covered by this figure.
- AD and BC are the line segments each equal to the radius of the given circle. Now, D is closer to P than in the previous case. Similarly B is closer to Q than before. This means that the curvilinear lengths DC and BA are coming closer to a straight line of length πr.
- Students may repeat the above procedure to divide the circle into more and more parts and place the parts side by side to get a figure such that:

  - Two sides AD and BC are equal to the radius of the circle. AB and DC becomes straight line of length πr.
  - Consequently the figure obtained by placing the parts of the given circle side by side almost coincides with the rectangle ABCD, whose lengths AB and CD are equal to πr and breadth AD and BC are equal to r.

Hence, Area of the given circle = Area of the parts.

= Area of rectangle ABCD

= AB × BC

$= \pi r \times r$

$= \pi r^2$

(Here r is the radius of circle)

9.3.20 *Surface Area of the Cone*

Rule: Surface area of the cone = p*rl*

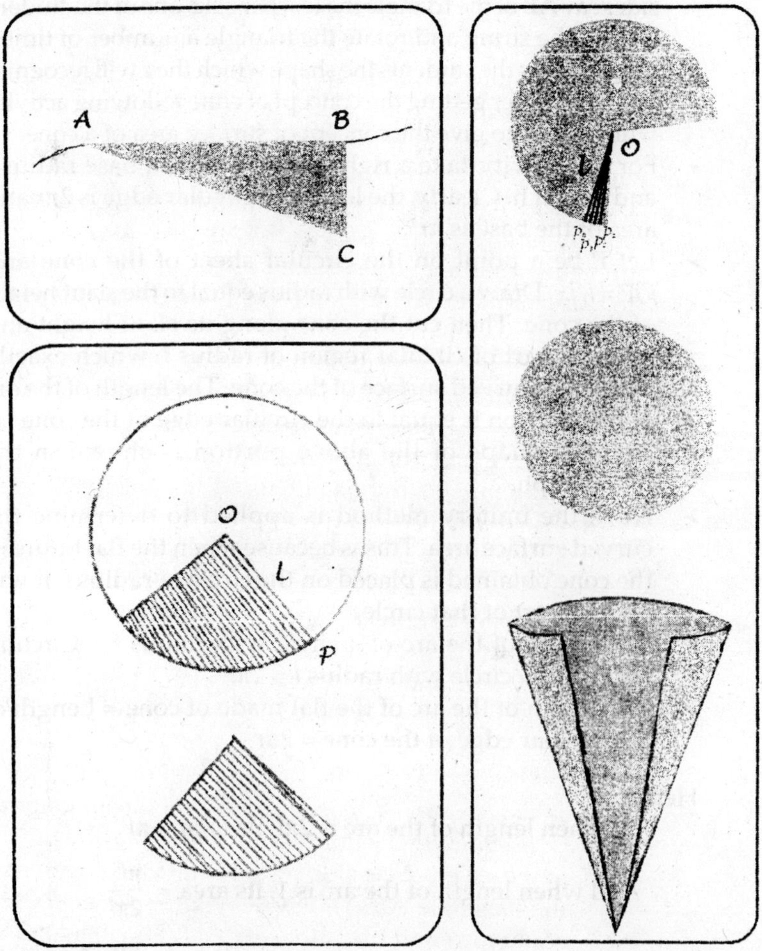

Activity

(i) *Material Required*: Sheet of paper.

(ii) *Description of the Activity:*

This concept is tough, but can be taught easily with the help of the following activity:

- To begin with, the teacher will explain the making of a cone by cutting out a right angle triangle ABC right angled at B. On pasting a long thick string along one of the perpendicular sides say AB of the triangle the teacher asks one of the student to hold the string and rotate the triangle a number of times. Then he asks the students the shape which they will recognise as a cone. After getting the concept of cone following activity will be done to give the concept of surface area of a cone.
- For the activity, take a right circular cone of base radius r and height h. Clearly, the length of circular edge is $2\pi r$ and area of the base is πr^2.
- Let P be a point on the circular sheet of the cone and OP = l, *i.e.* Draw a circle with radius equal to the slant height of the cone. Then cut the cone along its slant height and obtain a part of circular region of radius l, which exactly covers the curved surface of the cone. The length of the arc of this portion is equal to the circular edge of the cone *i.e.* $2\pi r$. The shape of the above portion is shown in the photograph.
- Now, the unitary method is applied to determine the curved surface area. This is because when the flat figure of the cone obtained is placed on the circle of radius l, it will cover a part of that circle.
- The length of the arc of a circle with radius l = Circumference of a circle with radius $l = 2\pi l$
- The length of the arc of the flat made of cone = Length of the circular edge of the cone = $2\pi r$

Hence,

When length of the arc is $2\pi l$, its area = πl^2

And when length of the arc is 1, its area = $\dfrac{\pi l^2}{2\pi l}$

When length of the arc is $2\pi r$, its area = $\dfrac{\pi l^2 \times 2\pi r}{2\pi l} = \pi rl$

Thus, the area of the portion of the circle of radius l, which exactly covers the curved surface of the cone, is equal to πrl. Thus, Surface area of the cone = πrl.

Where r is the radius of the base of the cone and l is the slant height of the cone.

9.3.21 Total Surface Area of Cuboid

Rule: Surface Area of Cuboid = 2 ($lb + bh + hl$).

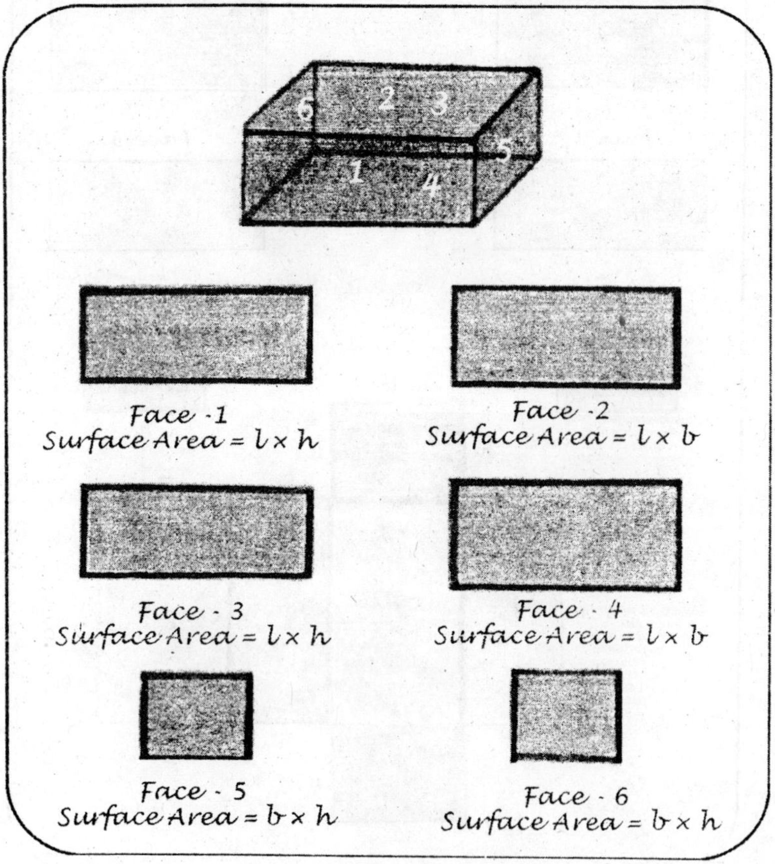

Fig. 1.

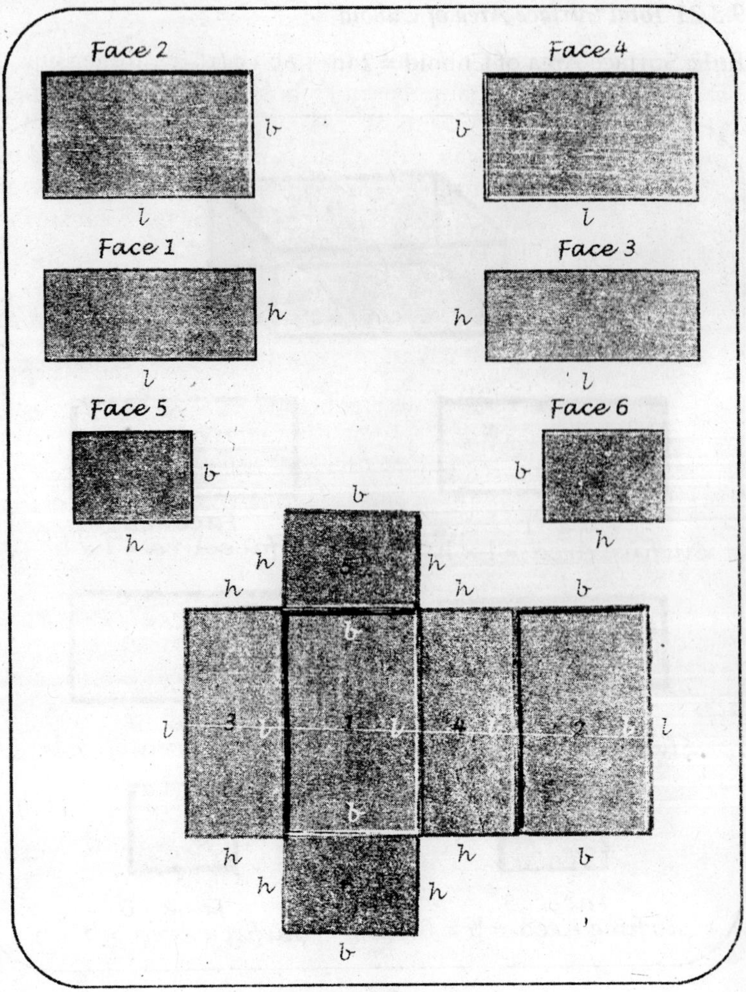

Fig. 2

Activity

(i) *Material Required*: Thick sheet of paper.
(ii) *Description of the Activity:*

To find out the surface area of a cuboid: A cuboid was shown to the students. The length, breadth and height of the cuboid were marked by different colour. Firt, the face no. 1 was shown and the students were asked about the shape and the dimension of this face, which was rectangular and whose dimension was length and height and the students were asked to find out its area. Similarly second face was shown and same question was asked. After finding out the surface area of all six faces, the areas were added up to calculate or derive the formula for the total surface area of a cuboid (Fig. 1).

This concept can also be given like this:

- The teacher showed six rectangular pieces to the students. Two of them have the dimension $l \times b$, two have $l \times h$, and two have $h \times b$ as shown in photograph.
- The teacher then shows how all these rectangles joined together can form in to a cuboid as shown in figure.
- Thus, total surface area of cuboid = Area of rectangle 1 + Area of rectangle 2 + Area of rectangle 3 + Area of rectangle 4 + Area of rectangle 5 + Area of rectangle 6.
- Total Surface Area of Cuboid

$$\begin{aligned}&= l \times b + l \times b + l \times h + l \times h + b \times h + b \times h\\&= 2 \times l \times b + 2 \times l \times h + 2 \times b \times h\\&= 2\,(l \times b + l \times h + b \times h)\end{aligned}$$

Thus, Total Surface Area of Cuboid = $2\,(l \times b + l \times h + b \times h)$.

9.3.22 *Volume of Cuboid*

Rule: Volume of Cuboid = $l \times b \times h$.

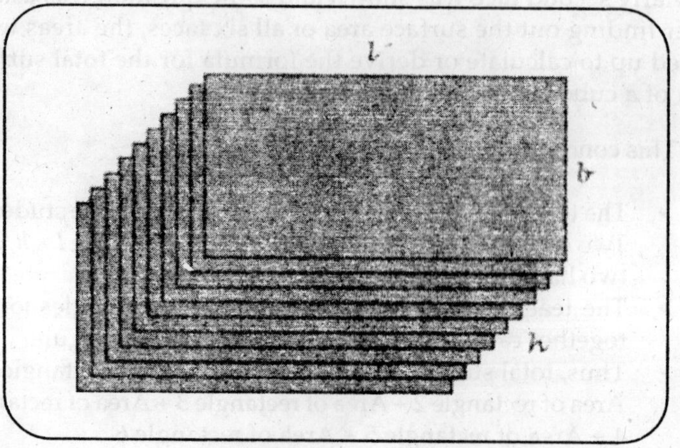

Activity

(i) *Material Required*: Thick sheet of paper.

(ii) *Description of the Activity:*

The following activity is an interesting and easy way to give this concept:

- First of all the teacher gives the concept of cuboid by showing a rectangular sheet of paper and explains if there is a bundle of these sheets then it will make a cuboid.
- After putting a rectangle on a table, the teacher asks how much space does it occupy. Students have the idea that this covered space is same as its area *i.e.* the area of rectangle = $l \times b$
- Now teacher places another same sized rectangle on the previous one. The total space occupied by these two rectangle = $l \times b + l \times b$.

The teacher displays a number of rectangles of same sizes and asks the students to place them on one another and calculate the total space occupied by all these rectangles. Students can easily find out this space as $l \times b + l \times b + ... + l \times b$. Now the teacher explains that, suppose there are '*h*' number of sheets placed one over the other of thickness 1 unit, then total space occupied by all sheets will be equal to volume of the Cuboid

$$= l \times b + l \times b + l \times b \,........ + l \times b \; (h \; times)$$

i.e. Volume of Cuboid $= l \times b \times h$.

9.3.23 *Construction of an Incircle in a Triangle*

Rule: To construct an incircle in the given triangle.

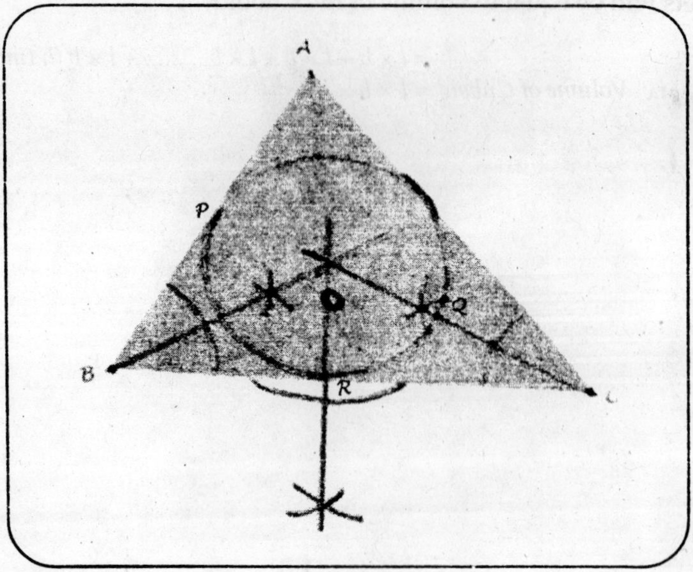

Activity

(i) *Material Required*: Thick sheet of paper, geometry box.
(ii) *Description of the Activity*:

To construct an incircle is a tough job in itself but it can be made simple with the help of the following activity:

- A thick sheet of paper and a cut out of a triangle is distributed to each student of the class and they are asked to paste the triangle on the thick paper sheet naming it as ΔABC.
- Then, they are asked to draw bisectors of any two angles of the triangle.
- Taking the point of their intersection as centre O and OP or OR or OQ as radius, they are asked to draw a circle. This will make the required incircle.

9.3.24 Construction of the Circum Circle of a Triangle

Rule: To construct a circum circle to the given triangle.

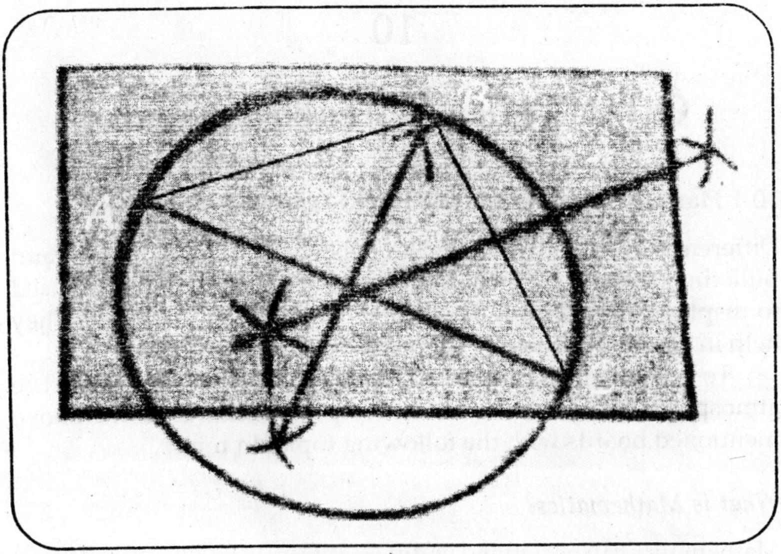

Activity

(i) *Material Required*: Thick sheet of paper, geometry box.

(ii) *Description of the Activity:*

To construct a circum circle is a tough job in itself but it can be simplified with the help of the following activity:

- A thick sheet of paper and a cut out of a triangle is distributed to each student of the class and they are asked to paste the triangle on the thick paper sheet and named it as ΔABC. (say).
- They are then asked to draw medians of any two sides of the triangle.
- Taking the point of intersection as centre say O and OA or OB or OC as radius they are asked to draw a circle. This will make the required circumcircle.

10

Other Types of Teaching Aids

10.1 Flannel Board, Magnetic Board, and Bulletin Board

Different types of boards like Flannel board, Magnetic board, and Bulletin board etc. are also important teaching aids. They are used to display charts with related information about any topic. They help in creating a teaching atmosphere in the classroom.

To create and maintain an interesting and educative atmosphere, the teacher can always put up charts on the above mentioned boards with the following topics in mind:

What is Mathematics?

Mathematics can be defined in different ways according to different levels of students, mental ability. Children's point of view is absolutely different from that of adult's. This concept can be represented through a chart on the bulletin board.

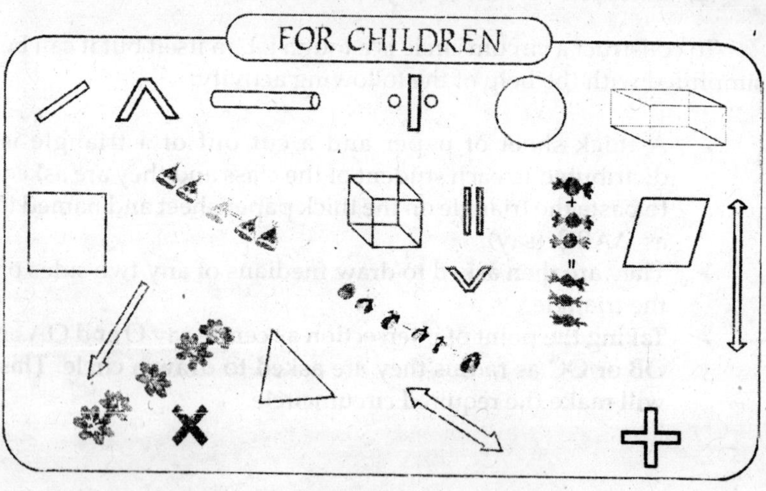

FOR ADULT

- Mathematics is the science of numbers and space.
- Mathematics is the science of measurement, quantity and magnitude.
- Mathematics is the science in which calculations are prime.
- Mathematics is a science of logical reasoning.
- Mathematics has its own language. This language consists mathematical terms, mathematical concepts, formulae.

Mathmatics in Daily Life

The use of mathematics in daily life can be represented on the bulletin board. Student can see it and can get the concept as to why it is necessary to learn Mathematics.

Number System

Charts about the number system can also be made and displayed in the classroom to give knowledge of the different number systems to the students.

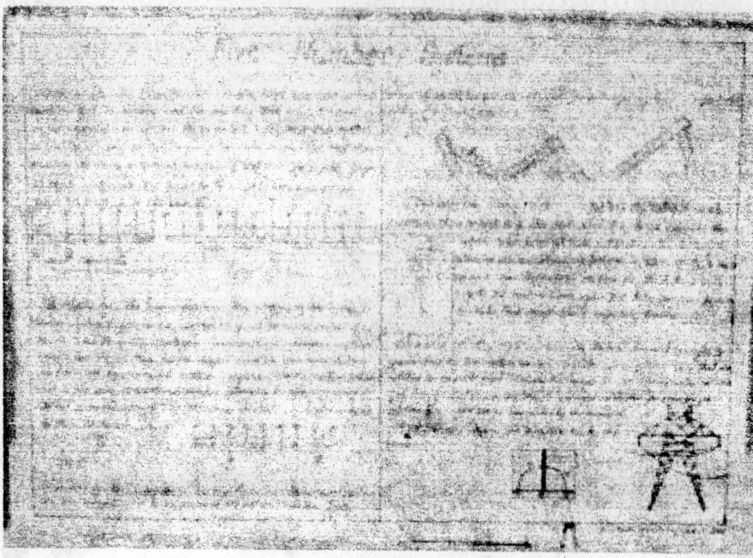

10.2 Computers

It is the latest addition to the list of modern teaching aids. The use of computers is becoming more popular in science and mathematics education in the field of educational technology. A computer is such a device which can cater to the needs of the individual learners by storing a large amount of information. It can process the information suiting to the needs of the individual learner. It can cater to a great variety of educational needs that range widely with respect to educational levels, subject matter, style of instruction and level of learning from drill and practices to problem solving.

Computers and software are referred to as '*Computers-Assisted Instructions* (CAI)' when they directly provide instruction to the student. According to internatic.ıal Directory of Education CAI can be defined as, 'use of a computer to assist in the presentation of instructional materials to a student, to monitor learning progress, or to select additional instructional material in accordance with the needs of individual learners.

In a CAI system, the computer stores the lessons in memory and enters into a dialogue with the student. During the interaction the computer pre:ents information, invites answers to questions, maintains records of students responses, and provides feed back on performance. The system can also generate and store tests, provide study prescription, keep record of study paths and generate reports, of course, all the things a good teacher can do.

A multimedia presentation of a lesson will be more effective and interesting than any other way of presenting a lesson. There are Compact Discs (CDs) prepared by experts available in the market.

Teachers can prepared their lesson themselves also. They can use the graphic facility which is a powerful aid in enhancing intuition, especially in giving insight into mathematical formulas and geometrical constructions.

The steps involved in the preparation of the lesson for CAI are as follows:

(i) Stating the objectives.
(ii) Structuring and organising the lesson pedagogically.
(iii) Writing the programme.
(iv) Editing.

Some examples of lessons made by teachers are as follows:

Lesson No. 1
CONSTRUCTION OF TRIANGLES
Class—VII

Objectives of the Lesson

After this lesson pupils will be able to:

1. Define all types of congruence conditions.
2. Differentiate between all types of congruence conditions.
3. Draw different types of triangles using given type of congruence condition.
4. Appreciate the use of computers in making understanding of constructions clear.

Previous Knowle dge

- The sum of the angles should be 180°
- The sum of any two sides of the triangle should be greater than the third side.

Condition No. 1

Triangle Construction by SSS Condtion

Given : ΔABC; AB = 4.5 cm, BC = 5 cm, CA = 6 cm

Steps of Construction

1. Draw a line segment BC = 5 cm.

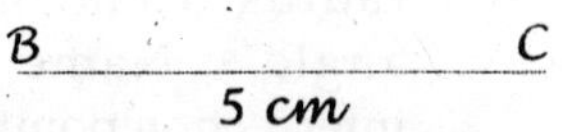

2. Taking B as vertex and radius of 4.5 cm, draw an arc.

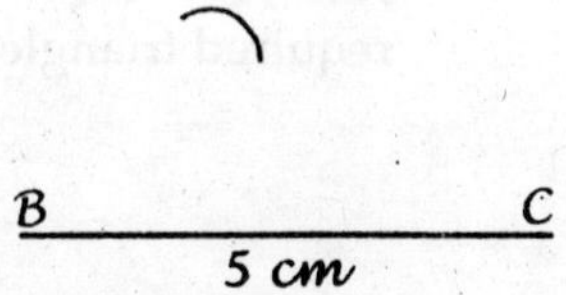

3. Taking C as vertex and radius of 6 cm, draw an arc cutting the previous arc at . Join A to B and C.

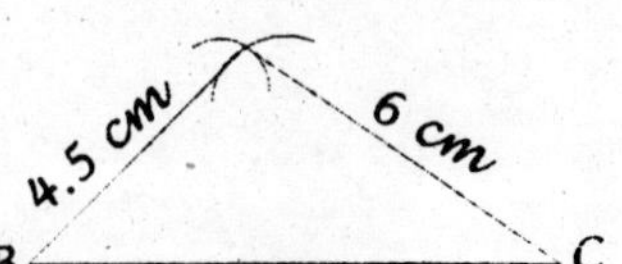

Condition No. 2

Triangle Construction by SAS Condition

Given: PQR; PR = 5 cm, ∠P = 70°, PQ = 3 cm.

Steps of Construction

1. Draw a line segment PR of 5 cm.

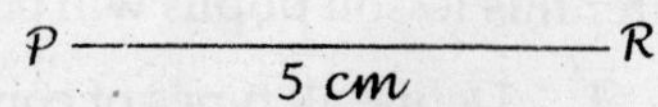

2. At P Draw an angle of 70°.

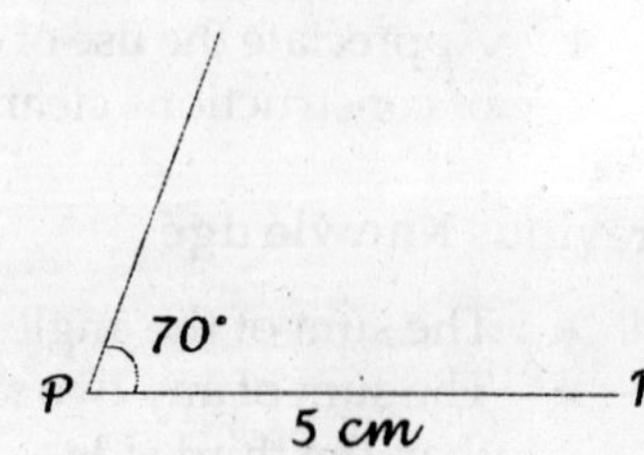

3. Taking P as vertex and radius 3 cm on the angle. Name the intersection point as Q. Join QR. PQR is the required triangle.

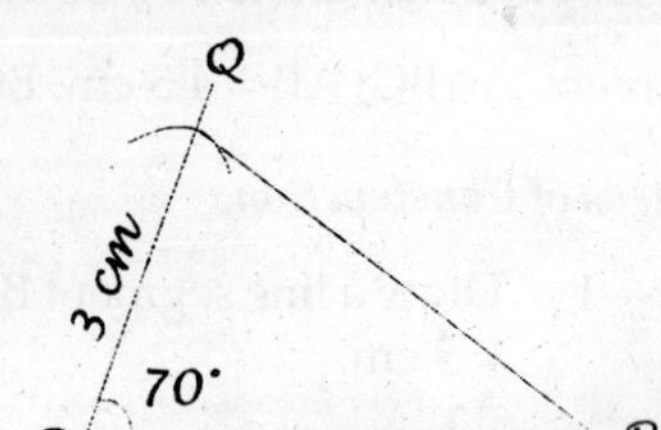

Condition No. 3

Triangle Construction by ASA Condition

Given: ΔABC; ∠A = 50°, ∠B = 70°, AB = 4 cm

Steps of Construction

1. Draw a line segment AB of Length 4 cm.

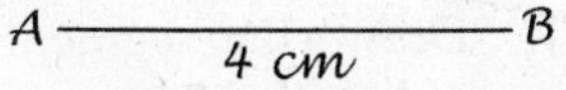

2. At A Draw an angle = 50°

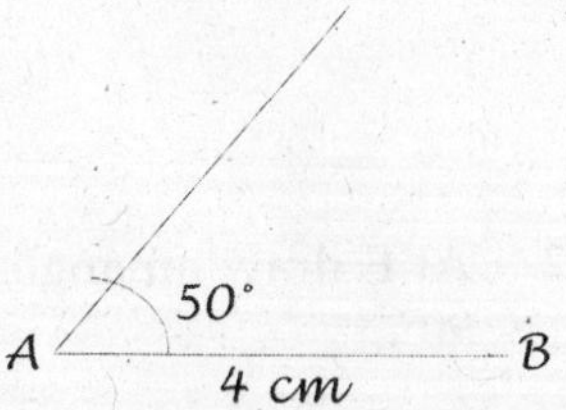

3. At B Draw an angle = 70° Cutting the previous angle at C. ΔABC is the required triangle.

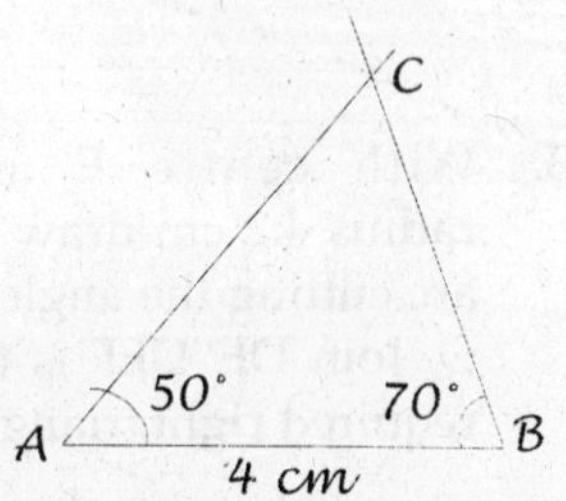

Condition No. 4

Triangle Construction by RHS Condition

Given : Hypotenuse DF = 4.2 cm; E = 90°, EF = 3.8 cm

Steps of Construction

1. Draw a line segment EF of length 3.8 cm.

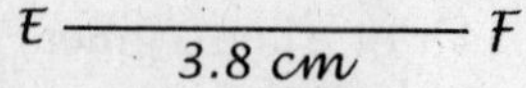

2. At E draw an angle of 90°.

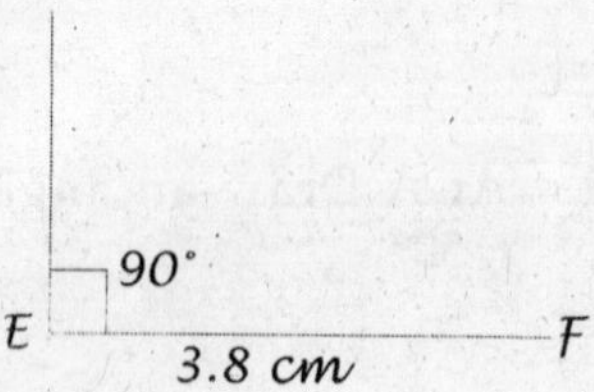

3. With centre F and radius 4.2 cm draw an arc cutting the angle at D. Join DF. DEF is the required right triangle.

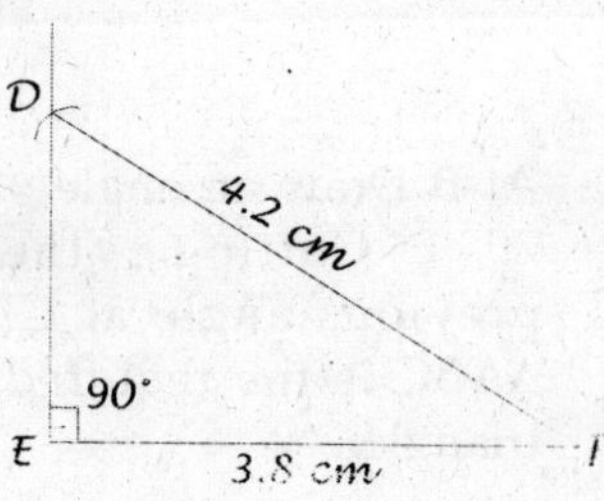

Lesson 2
TOTAL SURFACE AREA OF CYLINDER

Class—VIII

Specific Objectives in Behavioural Terms

After this pupil will be able to

- State the formula for C.S.A. of cylindeter.
- Derive the formula.
- Solve the related problems.

Previous Knowledge

Students are Expected to Know

- Area of rectangle
- Circumference of circle
- Shape of cylinder

Introduction

Some related questions can be asked to check the previous knowledge, like:

Q. What is the area of Rectangle?
Q. What is the Circumference of circle?

Concept of cylinder and its parts can be given by showing their pictures and discussing it.

This is a Cylinder.
Having a curved surface and two circular flat surfaces.

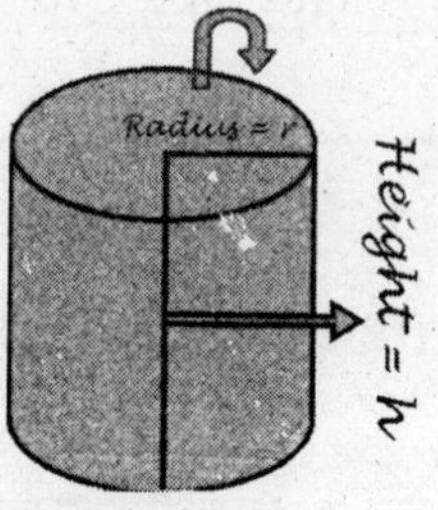

Q. What is the shape of this Figure?
Q. What will be its area?

When we fold this rectangle, see what will happened.

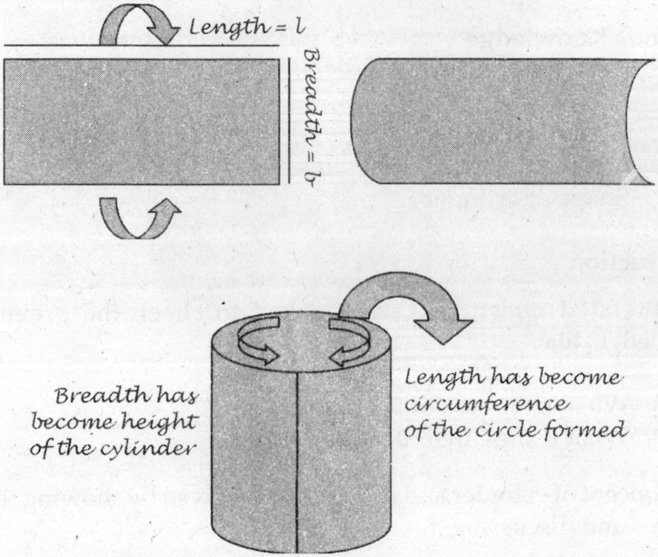

Q. What shape is formed?

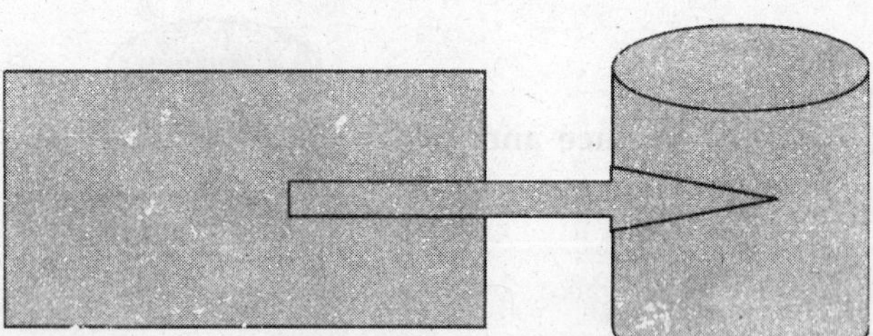

The surface of the Rectangle has become the curved surface of the cylinder. i.e. surface area of rectangle = Curved surface area of cylinder.

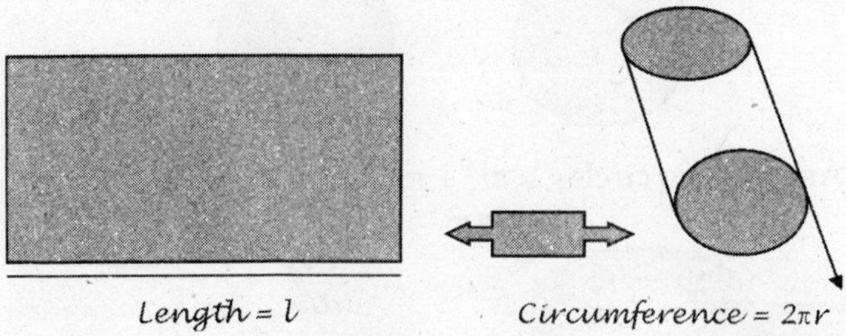

Length of rectangle = circumference of circle

$$l = 2\pi r$$

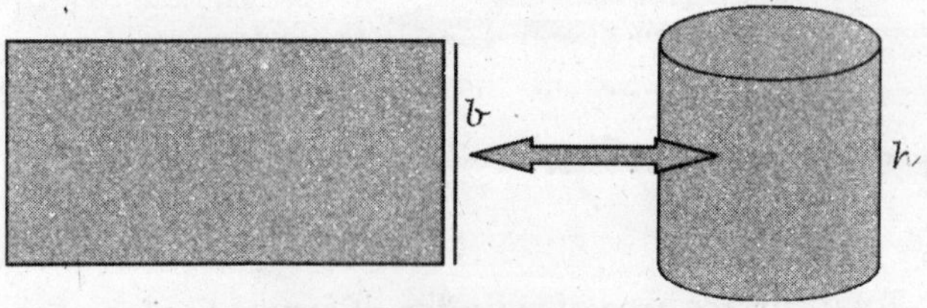

Breadth of the rectangle = Height of Cylinder

$$b = h$$

Therefore,

$$\begin{aligned} \text{C.S.A. of Cylinder} &= \text{Area of rectangle} \\ &= l \times b \\ &= 2\pi r \times h \\ &= 2\pi rh \end{aligned}$$

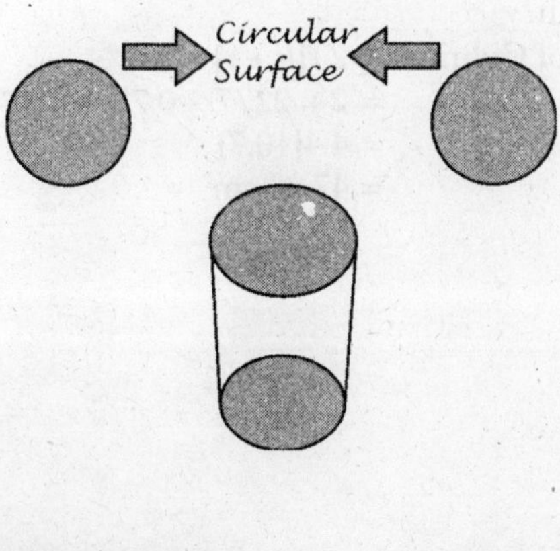

Adding areas of two circular surfaces to the curved surface area we will get total surface area of the cylinder.

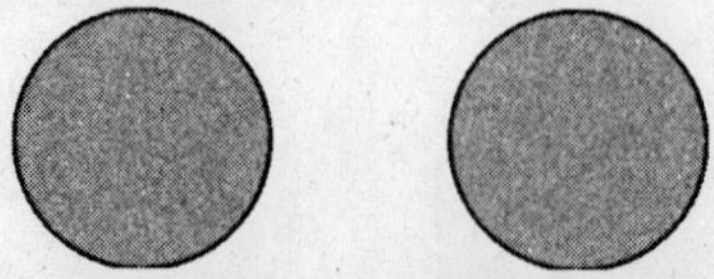

$$\text{Area of two circles} = \pi r^2 + \pi r^2$$
$$= 2\pi r^2$$

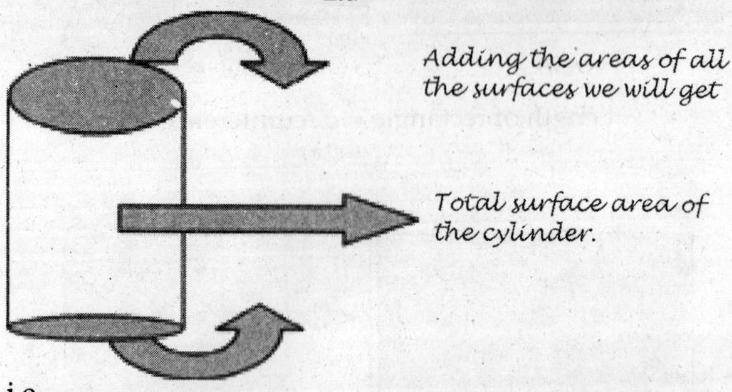

i.e.,

Total surface area of cylinder = Curved Surface Area + Areas of Two Circles
$= 2prh + 2pr^2$
$= 2pr\,[h + r]$

A Problem can also, be solved on computer to show the application of above formula.

Q. What is the T.S.A. of A Cylinder of Height = 10 cm, Radius = 0.7 cm?

Ans. T.S.A. of Cylinder $= 2\ r[h + r]$
$= 2 \times 22/7 \times 0.7[10 + 0.7]$
$= 4.4[10.7]$
$= 47.08\ \text{cm}^2$

Lesson 3
ALGEBRAIC IDEALITY

Class—VIII

Specific Objectives

After the lesson the students will be able to state the identity

- *Identify* the identities.
- *Compute* the identities with the help of an activity.
- *Solve* the problem based on this identity.

Previous Knowledge

- Students know $(a - b)^2 = a^2 - 2ab + b^2$.
- Students know the different types of identities.
- Students know $(a + b)^2 = a^2 + 2ab + b^2$.
- They can recall the areas of square and rectangle.

Introduction

- $(a + b)^2 = ?$
- $(a - b)^2 = ?$
- $(a + b)(a - b) = ?$

Consider a rectangle ABCD Whose length is $(x + b)$ and breadth is $(x + a)$, so the area of this rectangle is $(x + a)(x + b)$.

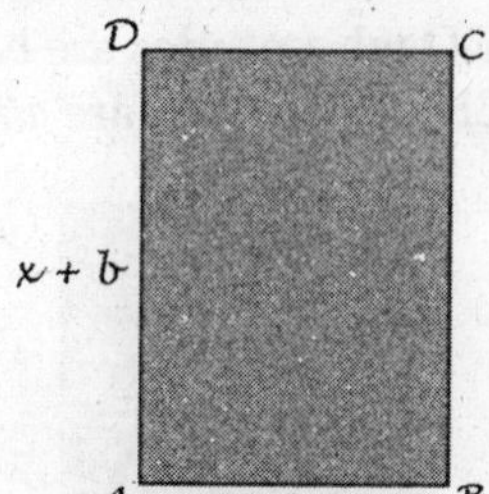

Take a point P on AB, so AP = x and take a point Q on AD, so AQ = x. Because AB = $x + a$ and AD = $x + b$. Therefore PB = a and QD = b.

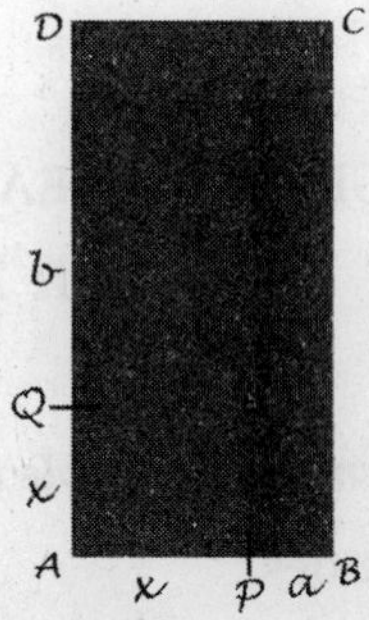

Draw two lines from P and Q which are parallel to AD and DC respectively and meet at R on the line DC and meet at S on BC.

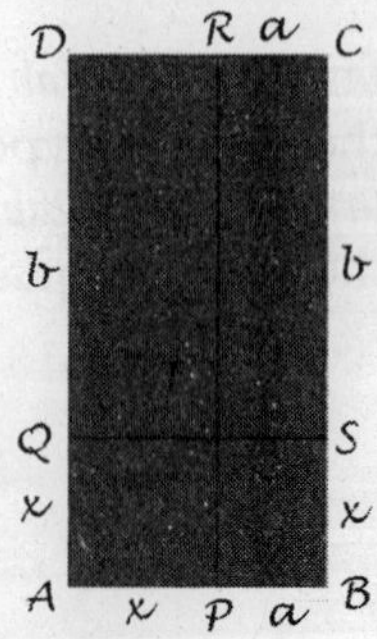

Now, the rectangle is divided into four parts:

1. Square APTQ whose side is x and area = x^2
2. Rectangle PBST whose sides are a and x so the area = ax
3. Rectangle QTRD whose sides are b and x so the area = bx
4. Rectangle TSCR whose sides are a and b so the area = ab

Cut along the lines PR, QT and TS and separate rectangles PBST, QTRD, TSCR and square APTQ.

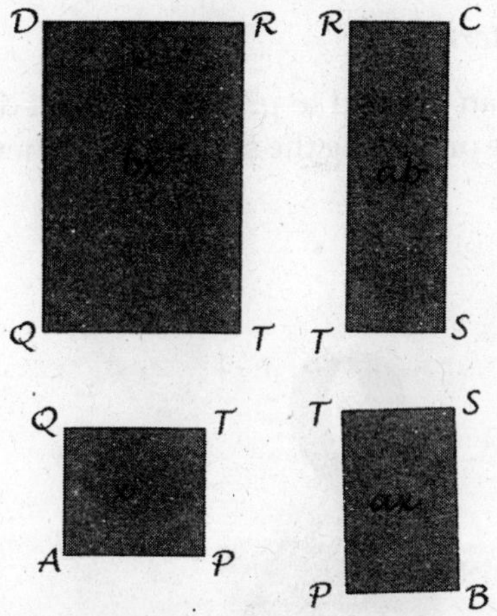

So the area of the whole figure is equal to the sum of the areas of the separate figures:

$$\begin{aligned}(x + a)(x + b) &= x^2 + ax + bx + ab \\ &= x^2 + (a + b) \times ab\end{aligned}$$

Recapitulation

Solve the following problems with the help of this identity:

1. $(y + 2)(y + 6)$
2. $(y + 5)(x - 3)$
3. $(z - 1)(z - 8)$

Home Work

Solve the following problems:

1. $(x + 4)(x + 5)$
2. $(x + 8)(x + 7)$
3. $(x + 4)(x + 9)$
4. $(x + 2)(x + 6)$

10.3 Projective Aids

Following projective aids can be used for this category:

10.3.1 Magic Lantern

A magic lantern can be used to project different diagrams, results, pictures etc. While projecting the slides the teacher can also explain the related things.

10.3.2 Filmstrip Projector

A filmstrip projector can be used to project the filmstrips on the screen. It is generally a hand-operated device. It contains a number of pictures drawn on a 35 mm or 16 mm film.

10.3.3 Epidiascope

This device can be used to project transparent as well as opaque pictures. It can be used to project slides, filmstrips etc. It can also be used to project the contents, figures and diagrams of the printed or written pages. It is quite useful for depicting complicated figures.

10.3.4 Motion Pictures

Motion Pictures are useful if we want to show action or motion. Such pictures are used to stress the publications of mathematics and development of concepts and generalization. Such pictures are capable of introducing real life situation in the classroom.

10.4 Radio

In these days we have regular programmes on radio, intended for school and college students. Listening to these educational programmes on radio would help in understanding the nature of the audio programmes. It is also possible to provide enrichment programmes in mathematics as well as on other different topics of various subjects through radio. A radio programme guide can be used to select the programme recording. For better result students can be given an outline of what to listen, and should be instructed to take notes.

10.5 Television

It combines the best element of the radio and the potentialities of a film. Students can benefit a lot if proper arrangements are made to show these T.V. programmes to the students.

10.6 Excursions

Excursions are helpful in providing the knowledge of mathematics and in developing interest and understanding of the subject. For such excursions students can be taken to a post office, bank, market, insurance office etc.

Bibliography

1. Agarwal, S.M. (1994). *A Course in Teaching of Modern Mathematics*. Dhanpat Rai and Sons, Delhi.
2. Anastasi, Anne (1966). *Psychological Testing*. New York. Macmillan Co.
3. Ausabel, D.P. (1966). Meaningful Reception Learning and the Acquisition of Concept. In Klasmeier, H.J. and Harris, C.W. (Eds.) *Analysis of Concept Learning*. New York & London Academic Press.
4. Berlyne, D.E. (1965). *Structure and Direction in Thinking*. Jhon Willeyand Sons, Inc., New York.
5. Bhandarkar and Wilkinson (1991). *Methodology and Techniques of School Research*. Himalaya Publishing House, Delhi.
6. Bhatnagar, B.A. (1985). *New Dimension in Teaching of Mathematics*. Modern Publishers, Meerut.
7. Bigge, M.L. (1971). *Learning Theories for Teachers* (Second Edition). Harper and Row, U.S.A.
8. Bloom, *et. al.* (1956). *Taxonomy of Educational Objectives Books I-Cognitive Domain*. Longman Green and Co. Ltd, London.
9. Busamma, K. (1993). *The Effect of Simulation Technique in the Teaching of Mathematics*. Indian Educational Abstract No. 5-8, 1998-2000.
10. Colier, C. Calhom & Learch H. Harold (1976). *Teaching Mathematics in the Modern Elementary School*. The MacMillan Company Collier Limited.
11. Dececco, J.P. (1970). *The Learning and Instruction*. Prentice-hall of India Ltd., New Delhi.
12. Eggen, P.D., Kauchak, D.P. & Harder, R.J. (1979). *Strategies for Teachers Information Processing Models in the Classroom*. Englewood Clifs, Prentice- Hall; Inc., New Jersey.
13. Gagne, R.M. (1983). *The Condition of Learning* (3rd Ed.) Holt. Saunders, International Editions, Printed in Japan.

14. Government of India: Ministry of Education, *National Policy on Education* (1968).
15. Government of India (1992). *Programme of Action.*
16. Joyce, D. and Well, M. (1960).
17. NCERT: National Curriculum Framework for School Education.
18. NCERT: National Curriculum Framework for School Education.
19. Piaget, Jean (1965). *'How Children Form, Mathematical Concepts'*, New York.
21. Simon and Sehuster. *The World of Mathematics*, New York.
22. Smith, D.E. (1900). *The Teaching of Elementary Mathematics*, MacMillion.

Index